# DEAR FRIEND
# I LOVE YOU

## Mary Katherine MacDougall

**CSA PRESS**
**Lakemont, Georgia 30552**

Standard Book Number 0-87707-226-4

Printed for the publisher by
CHB Printing & Binding, Lakemont, Georgia 30552

*Dear Friend, I Love You* is dedicated to C.R. Shelton, who is a dear friend.

# Table of Contents

| Title | Page |
|---|---|

| Title | Page |
|---|---|

| Title | Page |
|---|---|

| Title | Page |
|---|---|

| Title | Page |
|---|---|

Dear Friend,

This book is written as a continuing letter to you. We all like mail and this book is a daily letter. We all need friends. Sometimes we feel alone. Our friends may be out of reach. We may be in a strange place and have no new friends yet. We may be a person who has difficulty making friends. We may feel we don't have a friend in the world. We have two, You have me. You have the "I" of you, the Self of you, the God in You that is not only in you but all around you loving you all the time, wanting to do loving friend things. When you read the words, "I love you," "You are loved" and "God loves you," you will be reminded that you are loved all the time no matter how you feel, no matter what you think about yourself. We can never be alone, never be without friends. So, remember, God loves you, I love you, and you are loved.

*I love you,*

*Mary Katherine*

Mary Katherine

## Greater Than I

Dear Friend,

Today we remember how we felt as little children. We knew we were small in size, but we were safe because there was someone larger to take care of us. There still is. We may feel inadequate. We may feel helpless and alone. We may feel afraid. We had moments during childhood when movement of curtains was more than that and shadows on the wall were not from branches outside. We needed someone bigger and stronger. Above all we wanted someone who always loved us, to whom we could always run for comfort and reassurance. We still do.

And we still have that someone greater, someone who knows all. We need to know someone who can help us in every way. As we had our physical mother and father, so big, so everything for us, we have our Father-Mother God, all knowing, all caring, all providing. It's good to feel as a little child, to feel the instinctive turning to this Greater than we, this childlike trust and faith, this child knowing that all is going to be all right because we have this Greater than we.

Today we say often, "I am a little child. I am protected every way. I am guided and directed every way. I am provided for every way. I am always loved by my Father-Mother. No matter what, I can turn to my Father-Mother. I always have this greater than I am."

There is always this loving Greater than we. Today we rejoice that this is so.

## Always God

Dear Friend,

We are never alone because we always have God with us. We are never alone when we try to do the right thing. God is always with us making us a majority. Sometimes we feel alone and as if all the world is against us. We may feel that all of this world opposing us is wrong, and wrong seems to be succeeding. We can relax, we can be assured. Right, the good and desirable, is going to come through because right and good are the real and indestructible.

Wrong cannot last. It has no reality to last. It is unlike God, good, and God is the only reality. The wrong and undesired are only facts and facts change. Today we think and say to ourselves many times, "God is with me. God is with me. The power of good is with me, always with me. I am not alone. God is with me and together we make the majority for good."

The strength of the not good will lessen. We will feel our own strength for good increasing. As we stay with knowing we cannot be alone, things will change, the not right will get taken care of in ways that we don't have to plan. All we have to do is remember we are never alone.

"God and I are always a majority, a majority for good." How good!

# God Loves Me

Dear Friend,

Knowing God's love I cannot feel down or depressed today. I tell myself over and over that God loves me. God loves me. God loves me. The first thing I feel after I say this is that I am more comfortable. Comfortable, physically, mentally and emotionally. Very comfortable. God loves me. Then I feel happier. God loves me. How could I be anything but happy? I feel capable. How could I be anything but capable to do all I have to do? God loves me. I feel good things coming, coming closer and closer to me. They have to come. God loves me. Health is coming, has to. God loves me. Prosperity is coming, has to. God loves me. My job is coming. God loves me. My house is sold. God loves me. My new home is ready. God loves me. I have new friends. God loves me. I am not afraid. How can I be? God loves me. I make my peace with my antagonist. There is no other way. God loves me. I am strong. I have God's strength and God loves me. I make my decisions easily and wisely. I can. God loves me.

How wonderful it is, how perfect everything becomes when we know and declare that God loves us. We give thanks every moment for this love that takes care of everything and we give God our love today, and we say and say and say, "God loves me and I love God. God and I love each other." Today I know it all through me and I never forget it. God loves me and I love God.

15

## God Needs Me

Dear Friend,

There is only one thing God needs. Maybe we don't think God needs anything but God does. He has a great need. What God needs is us. We are very important to God. Without anyone of us, His world is not complete. We are necessary for the outworking of His plan for the world, not only for the completion of the plan for us.

How else can He be expressed in this world? How else can His work be done? How else can His joy be felt? How else can His peace be established? How else can His love be sent out to bless and heal His world? Only through us. Only through you. Only through me. Only through all of God's children everywhere.

Sometimes we don't feel we're necessary for anyone. We think that everything would go on whether we were here or not. It would go on, but it would not go on in the special way that it can go on with our help, without our doing, without our expressing God in our own special way. We can be no judge of what we do. All God wants us to do is what we can do so we stop thinking little and big. We simply do what we can do and we do it with joy and with excitement and enthusiasm, for it is exciting to know that we are important to God, that God needs us.

What beautiful words. God needs us. God needs you and God needs me.

## I Love You, God

Dear Friend,

What is one of the happiest ways we can wake up? To wake up with the words and feelings of "I love You, God," is the happiest way we can wake up. Thinking the words, feeling our minds and lips form them and feeling our heart giving them life, creates a song of gratitude and expectancy.

It is gratitude for the goodness of the night's rest, the protection, the comfort, the renewal of sleep. Expectancy of both expected and unexpected good, for that is what love does. Love expects continuous good. It is also gratitude for the happiness we feel in loving God.

Love is always happy with what is now because love is now. Love knows no past, no future, only now. Now is wonderful, beautiful, happy, glorious. So with our love for our Father-Mother God. Such content, such ecstacy, such satisfaction, such exhilaration. Love is now. Love content in the now does not fear or dread the future. Love knows love can take care of the future. Love is strength, love is faith. Love is knowing. Love is the promise fulfilled and fulfilling.

Our love for our Father-Mother God meets and blends with the love of our Father-Mother God for us. It is the moment sublime when we awaken each morning with the words, "I love You, God," on our lips.

## Immanent and Transcendent

Dear Friend.

The words "God Immanent" or "Immanent God" coupled with "Transcendent God" or "God Transcendent" bother some of us. Immanent is the God close to us, the God in us, the God personal to us, the I AM of us while the God Transcendent is the God that is outside of us, all around us—above, behind, beneath, at either side, the God that responds to us, the God that fulfills for us outside of us, the God that can lift us up, can transcend us from where we are to where we want to be. Both Gods are, of course, the One God but it helps us to think of God in this way.

God is everywhere, the movement of God is a flow throughout the universe, and this means the flow is through us and all around us, for there can be no place without God. We need to have a feeling of personal God and we need to have a feeling of the responding God.

We can live more effectively this way. We like and need the comfort and assurance of the God within and the comfort and assurance that outside of us God is working for us bringing things about.

We recognize the two working together when an opportunity comes that we ourselves have had nothing to do about, or very suddenly we have an idea that gets us to that opportunity. The outside movement of God often has something for the God in us to do. It is united action. Right now we give thanks for our God Immanent and our God Transcendent, one God, one Father-Mother of us all.

# No Shouting

Dear Friend,

God does not shout "Here am I." God does not blow trumpets and say, "This is the way you are to go. Get going." God does not make a display of Himself. God does not work noisily, flamboyantly. There is no bombast about God. There is stillness.

God manifests in stillness. It is in stillness that we meet God. It is in stillness that we can hear God. It is in stillness that God moves in us and it is in stillness that God moves in our outer circumstances. Inspiration, God speaking to us, comes quietly.

We may be doing something far removed from what we need help with and then there comes an idea, a God nudge —little, soft, quiet. God has told us what to do. When there is a definite need, it can be wise to take a nap, go to bed early giving thanks to our Father-Mother that the answer, God's answer, will come when we awaken. Sleep helps us still ourselves. We have to be still to sleep. Sleep helps us shut out all emotions. We are relaxed, we are in a state of receptivity. We are quiet and it is in quietness that God can move, that God can talk to us. Sometimes we awaken with a kind of gentle jerk, we may even exclaim, "Oh, that is the answer." God has spoken. God has indicated. No shouting, no trumpets, no fanfare. God speaks to us in stillness. We remember this and we take still moments.

## Today Is New

Dear Friend,

Today I know I am creating my world anew. Every day I create my world again. Each awakening in the dawn heralds a new day for me to create. Always creative with my thoughts and feelings and words I have a brand new day to create. There is nothing in my life that does not respond to and manifest what I creatively think and feel and speak about the new day and about everything and everyone in it.

I want a happy day so I do not create a miserable day by feeling miserable and saying so. I want a prosperous day, and I do not allow myself to feel poor in any way. Wanting a day of health and vitality I don't give my body sick directions. I may be the type that awakens with eyes open and body ready to go. I may be the type that takes awhile to come awake. It does not matter. With my first conscious thought I remember today is for me to create, to form, to make what I really want and I start creating.

I start by being thankful for sleep and for activity ahead. I start expecting happy, prosperous things to happen. This is the day that the Lord has made especially for me, and I welcome today as God's day creator. That is what I am. God has given me this day to create as I desire and I desre it to be good and I expect it to be good.

I'm creating today to be good and it will be.

## All Things New

Dear Friend,

Let us think today about the beautiful words, "Behold I make all things new." There are so many times when we want things new. There are times we want to make ourselves new. We have come in from outside activity and we feel dirty and tired. We take a shower and we emerge clean, new, refreshed, ready for the next activity. There is confusion in our office or home. We get it all cleaned up. Behold we have made these things new. There can be other conditions, circumstances that we feel unable to refresh, renew. But there is that of God in us, Christ in us, that can. Always we can turn within to this greater Self and know that we can make all things new. God in us can.

God that is within and without us can. All we have to do is turn whatever needs renewing over to God and then let God do it. Behold God. We don't tell God to bring about newness in any certain way. We wait, watch, behold God bring about the newness. Whatever needs renewing in our lives we give to God, we give to this high Self of us and then we expect and watch newness come. It always does.

We say many times today, "Behold I make all things new." God in us does.

## Today Only

Dear Friend,

Today is important because it is all I have. All I have is now. The past is gone and the future is not here yet. Often we allow ourselves to think so much of the past or the future that we miss out on right now. Today we are not going to miss out on a single bit of today's good.

We dismiss thoughts about past things unless there is something we must do about them. If so, we do them and think of them as now things. We don't let thoughts about future happenings absorb us. We think now, we think today.

No matter what today's weather is, it's O.K. for today. We adjust to it. We are going to be successful in everything that we are doing today. We can because we are concentrating on each job, each meeting, each happneing. We see the beauty of today, we feel the goodness of people and happenings. It's the most wonderful day of our life because it is the only day that we have now.

This is our day to be happy, to be successful, to be healthy, to be wise, to be loving. We don't miss a thing today. We don't put off doing things. We don't put off meditation and prayer. We thank God for this wonderful day that is ours today, this day that will not return. It's such a special day. We give it our love and our full attention. We give thanks for it.

## God's Way

Dear Friend,

Sometimes prayer results don't appear when and as we think they should. When this seems to be happening, we return to basics. God is the all Good, the all Knowing, the all Caring. God is all loving and God loves us. We think of this until we realize it with all our heart and being, not simply thinking it is so or may be. We are not only saying the words. We feel God's caring for us, loving us.

Then we ask ourselves, "Am I expecting God to work in this situation in the way I have planned? Have I been telling God what to do about me and my problem?" We are likely to discover that we have been doing precisely that. It can set us back on our spiritual heels. So we start again, remembering our all wise, all loving, all caring God.

We can trust God. We certainly can't trust ourselves to know what should be and what is best. So we give it to God. We pray, "Father-Mother God, take this condition (problem or situation). It is Yours to do with in the best way that only You know. It is safe with You. I know the solution (healing or demonstration) is coming in the right time, in the right way. I accept Your loving, wise solution. Thank You."

## God, Our Defense

Dear Friend,

God is our defense and our deliverer today. This is our prayer: "You, Father-Mother God, are our only defense, our only deliverer and we give thanks that You are."

It does not matter why we need to be defended, God is with us to defend us. It may be we need to be defended against criticism, against too much work, against feelings of lack, against anything that can be considered threatening to our welfare or to our peace of mind, threatening to our happiness or health, threatening to our success and prosperity. It may be that we need to be delivered from an uncomfortable situation, delivered from a worrisome time of indecision, or from a feeling of loneliness or one of drudgery. Perhaps even from a feeling that we are imprisoned.

We can be imprisoned in so many different ways. We can be self-imprisoned by depression, by memories. The defense and the deliverance that most of us need is from negative parts of us, emotions and thoughts and habits that we allow to keep us from our highest good. We know what they are.

Today we let God, our all loving Father-Mother God, defend us and deliver us from any and all negation that we are allowing to bind us in anyway and we give thanks that deliverance, that defense comes now.

God is our complete defense and deliverer today.

## God Accepts

Dear Friend,

God always accepts our invitation. God activity will come into our life and affairs, come into any situation or circumstance we may be concerned about, but we have to issue the invitation. It is part of free will, free determination of our life and affairs that God gave us in our creations. This is part of our right to choose. After we have given God the invitation to come into our life, we need to give God time and freedom to act in God's way.

Frequently, when we have invited God to come into our problem, we don't give God a chance. We keep on directing traffic in our lives. We don't stop and wait, expecting good to start happening. God activity hasn't a chance if we keep trying our way. If our way were best it would have already accomplished the need. We give up, we say, "God, take over. It's all Yours." When we give a party or want to play golf with someone, we give the invitation. Our invitations are not always accepted. Our invitations to God always are.

Then we do what any good host or hostess will do, let the guest be himself or herself and we let our Father-Mother God be the wonderful God Self and do the loving, beautiful things only our Father-Mother God can do. We remember we give the invitation and step back to let our all resourceful Guest decide and bring about what is best to happen. Today we invite God and God activity and we give fervent thanks that God always accepts our invitation.

"I invite God into my life and God comes."

## God Thoughts

Dear Friend,

Today I remember to invite God to think through me, to feel through me, to speak through me and to act through me. This is a wonderful thing to do when we awaken each day. It gets us in order for the day. It gets the day in order. It opens us up to the goodness of the day, opens us up to the possibilities for our making this day a very good day, which it already is unless we spoil it. When we have done this regularly we will find that we have an openness of mind and heart, we have a relaxed good feeling throughout us. We have put God in charge. We have put God in the director's chair of our day.

The day has to be good. God is good and with God in charge then the day is going to be the way it should be, very good. When we begin this we may find that we are not letting God be completely in charge of our thoughts and responses and our actions. We will have a divided feeling, part God directing, part our directing. This will pass. We will let our limited directing go, we will let God direct.

It will be a happy day because God's ways are happy. It will be a fulfilling day because God knows only richness. It will be a healthy day because God knows only wholeness and perfection. It will be a wise day because God's ways are ways of wisdom. It will be a wonderfilled day.

26

### Spiritual Progress

Dear Friend,

A friend of mine said she didn't think she was making spiritual progress. We all need to think positively about our spiritual progress. We know we are growing when we remember that God is in others, when we see God in situations. Even if we are having times when we don't remember to see God in others until later, even when we let our negative reactions of fear, disgust, criticism come first, we remember later that God has to be in all of these things. Despite our having times of darkness and doubt we have our moments of illumination.

These show us we are defintiely on our way so we can affirm many times today: "I am making spiritual progress as I see God in people and circumstances." Sometimes it seems we are decreeing things too great for us but we are not. We are only stating the truth about us. We are created to know God in everything for God is everywhere present. We are created to see God in all people. God has to be in everyone because God is in us and God is no respecter of people. We are being illuminated.

Every new truth that we take in is an illumination, for each new truth gives us light on our path to our promised perfection.. "I am seeing God in everyone, and in all happenings. I am illuminated." And we are and we will be more and more as we let our God vision expand.

# Knowing Us

Dear Friend,

An interesting experiment was carried out in a psychology class at North Iowa State University. Each student was given a lemon on Monday and was to keep that lemon with him or her all the time. Carry it wherever he went, take it to meals, in the car and sleep with it at night. It wasn't simply to be put in a pocket but carried, felt, handled. Friday, each student brought his lemon back to class.

This time instead of handling it during class, all the lemons were put into one container, stirred up and then each one was asked to take out a lemon, their own lemon. Each one selected the lemon he had been given! He had been with the lemon so closely that he knew it, knew its little differences from other lemons, knew its feel, knew its look.

Even if we cannot get away from ourselves, we rarely really stay with us in the way that these students did with lemons. How many of us really know ourselves, really know our peculiarities, our individual differences, know what we are actually like? Today we are going to consciously be aware of us, aware of the physical of us, the mental of us, the emotional of us, the spiritual of us. We will try to see us as we are. These students didn't criticize the lemons they had, they simply got to know them, to stay with them. That's what we are going to do. We'll find out much. It will be a day of revelation. It will be a day of appreciating our specialness. Good will come from our knowing us better.

## Self-Awareness

Dear Friend,

Together we think and pray about becoming more objective about ourselves. When we do, we learn how our mind is working, what our emotional responses and reactions do. One writer has said that until a consciousness is aware of itself it cannot expand. We can be sure that when we observe ourselves we start to expand our consciousness. We want to be aware of all the wonders of our physical self, all the wonders of our emotional and mental activities.

Today, with the help of God within, we observe all we are thinking, and feeling; we hear all we are saying. We become keen and loving observers of all we do. We will learn about us. We will find more than we may expect that is right and be pleased. We need to be pleased with ourselves.

When we discover negative reactions, unhappy patterns of thinking, we will stay objective, we will reroute our thinking and feeling. We won't get mad at ourselves, we won't get discouraged. We are becoming aware of ourselves so that we can be better in every way. We become onlookers. We observe our potential. We see what to encourage and what to change.

Thank God we are created so that we can know ourselves. We can change, grow and expand ourselves. We can become all we are created to be. This is our day of observing us and we will see that we are good. We will see that we are going to be better.

## Our 'Self'

Dear Friend,

How many thousands of times we have heard and read that we have to find out who we are. Many of us have gone through a period of being uptight about who we are and what we are to be about. We all know that we are more than vital statistics, more than name, sex, race, age, nationality, a person who lives at a certain address and does a certain job. More too than being a father or mother, a son or daughter, a grandparent, an uncle or aunt. More than being a high school drop out, college graduate, technician, doctor, lawyer. The real of us is more.

It is the Self of us that we know is there but haven't found. Perhaps we haven't named it Self with a capital S but we have felt It. We know It is there, something that is greater than facts, something that can get us to where we should go. This is our God Self, our divine Self, this is the Self of us that knows what we were created to be.

Today we invite our Self out into the open. We know It is there. We know It knows the answers. It knows who we are. Today we let our Self out. Amazing things will happen as we proclaim, "Today the real of me, my Self, comes forth. Today I meet my Self. Today I know my Self."

# Self-Determination

Dear Friend,

There is much talk and desire for self-determination. We all want and need self-determination. Each of us has specialness that needs to be allowed to grow. This specialness is God's plan for us. Of ourselves we can't know how best to let this Plan unfold. God knows so we let God show us the right way. Perhaps we do not know what we are to do.

Whether we do or not, we take time to be still, to dedicate this day to the Father-Mother's helping us with our self-determination. We know there is a special way for us to go. We will discover what it is for us to do and we want to become the best, the very best us. God will help us be the best us. God will help unfold the plan of our lives. God will help us do what will bring about our true Plan. Direction will come. Fulfillment will come.

No matter how cramped or stymied or frustrated we may feel, how deep in a rut of routine, today we can be free from all hindrances to our own specialness. It is a day of self-determination for us. It is a day of opening ourselves up to the wonder of becoming what we are created to be.

Today we give thanks for the real of us and know, "I am now free to be the real me. The real me unfolds now in perfect ways as God directs and helps. There is something special for me to do."

## Real of Me

Dear Friend,

Today I try in every way to be the real me of me. I do not let other people influence me to do things that I do not believe I should do or are not mine to do. I let the love that is in me come out even when it may not seem to be the time or the place for love to come out. I know the real me is loving. I know the real me is wise. I know the real me is strong. I know the real me is patient and kind. I know the real me is efficient and capable. I know that the real me knows what I should do and I do it. I find that as I think of being the real me that I am not tense. I am relaxed. I am confident. I feel sure. I am not afraid.

I am not concerned about how others are reacting to me. I am not afraid of what people may think or do or say to me or about me. I am with the real me, the part of me that is my God self. The part of me that is unfolding to become all the good that I was created to be. I give thanks for the real me of me. I give thanks for the specialness that is mine, the truly wonderful me that God created.

The real me is taking over. The hurt me, the angry me, the impatient me, the unkind me, the inadequate me, the me that lacked in confidence takes a back seat. Today I bring the real me out. I let the real me decide. It is wonderful to know there is this real of us and we give thanks for it.

## Seeds of Greatness

Dear Friend,

A poet has written that we carry within us seeds of something greater than we are now, greater even than we can imagine now, greater than we can dream, greater than we can possibly conceive now. There is in you and me a potential for such unlimited good, such unlimited achieving that we cannot know it, even in our most far reaching dreams. It is unlimited because it is God given and there can be no limits to what God has created in us and for us.

We may smile because we can't imagine this much great good but we think about it. We begin to know there is more for us to have, do and be. We thank God for creating in us the possibility He has given us and for the help He will give us.

Today we go about our day singing inside, "There are seeds of greater good inside me. There are seeds of greater achievement inside me. There are seeds of greater health, greater wisdom, greater joy." We nurture these seeds, we feed them with love and expectancy and faith and they will grow. We will feel them sprout, we will see signs of growth and we will know that they will bear fruit. There will be a harvest, a harvest we cannot envision now. We don't have to. We need only take care of the seeds.

## Celebration of Us

Dear Friend,

Today let's celebrate us, celebrate all that we have achieved. Celebrate all we've done, progress we are making because we are making progress. We cannot desire to know more about God and ourselves and our relationship together without becoming better, without seeing life more as it truly is, expecting good and more good to come into our lives and into the lives of everyone else. We are making progress and today we mark that progress.

This is a special day. This is our day of celebration of us. So today we think about how far we have come along in Truth's way, how far in Love's way. We don't waste one moment thinking that we still have far to go to be all that we are to become.

Today we don't think of the wonderful future of us but the wonder and the goodness and the love of us that is now. This is our day. Our day to rejoice and give thanks for us, give thanks for this person we are, this person God created in a special way. We praise all that we have accomplished without any thought of what we are going to do and be. Today marks our progress to date and we see that it is good and all day we celebrate what we have already become.

This opens us wide to new progress in our soul growth, in our health, wisdom, prosperity and joy. Today we celebrate us.

## My Own Everything

Dear Friend,

I am my own everything. You are your own everything. Everyone is his or her own everything. In us is everything we need because God is in us as well as all around us. Therefore, in us is all the wisdom we can need, all the strength and vitality, all the joy, all the ideas for our prosperity, all the love. Realizing this does not mean that we are shutting others out, it is making us stronger, better, even more attractive to others and better able to understand others, know how to help others, and, above all to love others. I am my own everything.

I am all right wherever I am. Wherever I am, I have all that I need. I can never feel lonely. I am my own center of love and joy. It is exhilarating to get the impact of this truth about us. *I am my own everything.* No more need to blame anyone for anything. No more need to worry. Nothing to fear. In me is everything including protection and the ability to make things right. In me everything I need! As we think about this and, as we think of why this is, we not only let God in us take care of us but we become more completely, and consciously one with God all around us, more completely one with our God, God we call both immanent and transcendent, God in us doing and God outside us transforming.

I am my own everything. We accept this, use its Truth, enjoy it, and let it be.

## No Limit

Dear Friend,

"All things I am, can do and be through Christ, the Truth, that is in me." This is the statement of Easter, and Easter is every day. This Truth can raise us up out of any dead situation, any guilt, remorse, hurt or disappointment.

The gospel accounts of the resurrection all begin with "early in the morning," and it is always early in the morning for us to change, always a new day lies ahead, new hope, new life, new strength, new love and happiness, new success. Newness, the newness of the dawn. The wonder of the dawn, the wonder of newness, the wonder of resurrection. Daily we can have our rising up, rising ever up out of whatever we have let bog us down, rising up to newness of every good kind. It is a glorious knowing, it is a glorious assuring.

Today we know we are rising up out of any limitation, rising up out of lethargy, procrastination. We are rising up from discouragement, fear and loneliness. We are rising up from lack and bondage of any kind. We are awakening to a new day. The darkness is going, the light is coming. Everything in our lives is becoming new.

"All things I am, can do and be through Christ the Truth that is in me."

## No Impossibility

Dear Friend,

God knows no impossible situation, God knows no incurable disease, God knows only the possible because God knows only good. God cannot know anything unlike good. If we know this, we may forget it in times of stress. We may think it is impossible to believe for we've been told so many times and in so many ways that there is impossiblity.

We start by saying often, "God knows no impossibilities." We say it whether or not we believe it. We want to believe it. We know God is all powerful and all good, all knowing and knows how to make everything good. Gradually the belief and the feeling of the truth of the words become part of us.

When the impossible or incurable concerns other people, we can give the most wonderful help by knowing for them that nothing is impossible to God. How the other person believes does not matter, that is not our concern. Our concern is to stay with, "God knows no impossibilities." This is the way to see perfection, to see divine order, to see good coming where good has not been, to see healing come, prosperity come.

Today and every day we know, we say, we believe and we are grateful for the truth for us and others that, "God knows no impossibility. God knows no incurable diseases."

## Child of Light

Dear Friend,

Let's think about the light that is in us, the light of the Christ that is in us, God's light. Jesus the Christ called us children of light and told us to walk in the light. It's wonderful that we are not children of darkness, that we cannot be children of fear, loneliness or lack, that we cannot be in the darkness of being unloved, unwanted, incapable or forgotten.

We have a feeling of light when we understand things. When we are happy there is a lightness of heart. When we feel good there is a brightness around everything.

Where does this darkness of light come from? It's a reflection of our own light, light we always have in us. Sometimes we pull our self shades down, sometimes we put blankets of self-pity, worry, and dread over our light. Today we are going to let our light shine for we are children of light. We are free to walk in the light of love and joy, understanding and wisdom, strength and energy, abundance of every good thing.

We can see our way only in the light, we can see our good only in the light. Today we see, today we keep our light shining. It is a day of light. We see who we are, see where we are going, we see our good everywhere. We give thanks for light in us, light all around us, light that is us. We say it, we think it, we feel it, we sing it: "I am a child of light and my world is bright."

# God Shines Through Us

Dear Friend,

Today God in you is shining through. Isn't this a beautiful truth to know about us? Isn't it a beautiful truth for us to know about everybody today? God in me is shining through right now. God in you is shining through right now. God in me is shining through me right now. God in you is shining through you right now. Wonderful, beautiful words, true words. We are going to sing them to ourselves all day, we are going to sing them to others. Our singing may not be heard by others as singing but it will be heard by others as love and enthusiasm and recognition of them as special. There will be a new and wonderful specialness about each of us as we tell ourselves, shout it to ourselves, sing it to ourselves, "God in me is shining through me today, this minute."

Our body cells will be stimulated because God in them is recognized and appreciated, our emotions will all be loving, happy, for God is being allowed to express through them today. People will respond, they will be happier, they will be given the greatest possible recognition and encouragement. The world will be happier for we will be helping all the world to know, to remember that God is in all, ready to shine through.

## Beyond Our Concerns

Dear Friend,

Today we are going to think beyond ourselves, beyond our families, beyond our friends, beyond our work. Oh, we will take care of our families, friends, and our work. We'll do our job but we will direct that other thinking we do while we are working. We will direct this thinking and feeling out beyond the regular. We will think out into the world and we will watch the thoughts going out.

It's vital that we do this. Our thoughts affect the world. Our thoughts and feelings about the world are very important to the way the world goes. Today we send out love. We send out blessings. We send out hope. We send out faith. We send out expectancy of good coming to every part of the world. We send out expectancy of good, wisdom, good sense, peace to every troubled spot. We then become the light of the world.

Our love and our blessings give the light that is needed everywhere. This is the way that we can go into the world to take tidings of great joy. Our belief that there is a better way to live, to govern, to do the world's business will help. These are wondrous things and they are gifts we can give today to the world as we go out beyond our immediate world and its activities and relationships and challenges. Our own world will be better for it. Whenever we look with eyes of love and blessings, love and blessings return to us. Today we send our thoughts out with love. We go beyond our own concerns. It will be a better day.

## The Great Support

Dear Friend,

We like to have support. We like it when we are walking over a shaky bridge. We like it when we are running for office. We like it when we want customer support. We like it when our family and friends stand behind us when we need them. Sometimes we don't give others support they need.

There are reasons. Sometimes we're afraid of what other people will think. Sometimes we don't know how to support. Sometimes we think that any support we can give is not enough. Maybe it's money and we can't give much. Some support we can always give.

Moral support. Prayer support. Prayer support is the greatest of all support and we can give it anywhere, any time, and in any quantity. It is true support, it is unlimited in effect. It is support that opens channels for the person we are supporting. It opens us and them up to ideas that will help. They will feel this support. They will be strengthened. They will be encouraged. They will be able to go on surer of their success or victory.

Prayer support can be given in the middle of the night, early in the morning, late at night, during the day. The beauty of prayer support is that it is not only support we give out to others but we give ourselves as well. We cannot give prayer support to anyone without receiving support for ourselves. This is the only support that surely brings support back to us.

## Prayer Check

Dear Friend,

Today we are going to check our prayers.

How are we praying? Are we pleading with God, are we shouting at God, are we telling God all about our problems? Or, are we thanking God for the answer to questions in our lives? Are we listening or simply reciting our woes? There are times when we need to cry out, to let our emotion, to let our fears, anxieties go out, but after we have let go of emotional steam, we need to remember that God knows the answers, the solutions. God is the answer and we get still so that God in us can direct us, open our eyes to the answer, open our hearts to understanding.

God knows what should be done, what can be done. God knows perfect outcomes. Today we stop being God informers. We become, instead, God listeners. Today we stop telling God our problems, we give thanks for and wait for solutions. We let God be our help in every need by letting God be what God is always for us—the answer, the solution, the direction, the opportunity, the assurance, the comfort, the healing, the provision, the everything we can possibly need.

Today is a joyous day. We will enjoy our prayer times more as we stop reciting our hurts and needs, our lacks and concerns and joyously, gratefully give thanks for our Father-Mother God who has the answers, who will show us the way no matter how dark it seems now.

God has the answer. We pray with assurance.

## Love Then Pray

Dear Friend,

It has been said that if we cannot love, we cannot expect our prayers to be answered. Jesus the Christ told us that if we had anything against our brother to get it straightened out before going to sleep. We need to get it straightened out before we pray. To not love closes prayer doors.

We know God is love. If we shut love out in any way, we shut God out and it is difficult to think of praying to a God we have shut out. Of course, God is not shut out. But we can close communications doors between God and us.

We do not want to shut love, God, out, so today we don't. Today we pray and pray easily for love makes everything easier. We shut no one out from our love. We keep all doors open to love.

We remember God is love and God loves. We are love and we love. Then prayers become more loving. We open up to perfect answers to our prayers for they are love prayers and love does everything in perfect ways.

Today we love. Today our prayers are love inspired, love desired, love fulfilled.

## Joyous Acceptance

Dear Friend,

When we pray today let's check to see if we are praying a prayer of acceptance or a prayer of beseeching. It makes a difference to the strength of our prayers if we are ready to accept answers, and have the feeling of accepting the good that we are praying about. It makes no difference what we are praying for, we need to pray our acceptance.

This is praying as Jesus the Christ told us to pray, to pray believing, to ask believing. Believing in the answer, knowing that the answer is coming, praying believing we will have our prayers answered and feeling that we are already accepting the answer. If we believe, in our minds and hearts, that our prayers will be answered we are accepting.

It is good for us to say many, many times, "I accept. I accept. I accept all the good God has for me now. I accept the answer as already here now. I accept the solution as already known. I accept the opportunity I need. I do not merely wish it. I accept. I accept. I accept my good now."

Today we give thanks to our Father-Mother God that good is ours, ours to ask for and ours to accept. This is the way to pray believing. This is the way to ask believing. Today we pray, accepting the answer, accepting the fulfillment.

## Meditation

Dear Friend,

Meditation brings us closer to God. Meditation is our time of perfect stillness. It is good to meditate regularly. Stillness gets us ready to be with the Lord of our being. This is our response to the Bible's repeated injunction, "Be still and know."

When we first read these words or hear them we may ask, what will we know? What can we know? What is there to know? When we are still we can listen, listen to what our Father-Mother God has to tell us. It is never the same for all of us. Your knowing will be different from mine. But all of us will know the Presence, the Presence that is always with us, but we may not recognize.

When we get still, it is wise to have in our minds a word or a phrase or promise or a statement that gets us ready to wait for the knowing that will come from our Indwelling Lord. Statements of love, peace, thanksgiving, strength, wholeness, praise or blessing of our Father-Mother are good. Thinking of a promise such as, "Lo, I am with you always" or "The Lord is my shepherd," also helps still our minds. We repeat our chosen words to ourselves as we get still. We repeat them again and then we are completely still. We let the words go. We are still and we know that knowing will come, renewed strength will come. Whatever we need will come. We are still and we listen and it is good.

## Contemplation

Dear Friend,

Contemplation is a beautiful word. It is a calming word. It is an unhurried word. It is a word that brings with it the thought of wisdom and understanding, of poise, of depth of thought. It is what we are going to practice and experience today. Today is to be our day of contemplation. These times do not need to be lengthy but they need to be still, quiet times.

We still ourselves and cease thinking about things to do or worries or concerns and we take one beautiful thought, one beautiful word, one beautiful picture, one beautiful memory, one beautiful dream and we exclude all else from our consciousness. We let the word or idea or picture or memory float through our mind, unhurried. We savor it. We look at all the details in a completely unhurried manner. We see it all and new details come to our inner sight, new feelings about it come. We become more still and continue to contemplate, look at, consider, love and appreciate what we are contemplating. Now understanding comes as we contemplate, bringing greater depth of feeling. Gently we thank our Father-Mother God for complete knowing about what we contemplated and still greater knowing comes. When we end our period of contemplation we will feel refreshed, we will feel new strength, new inner joy.

## Visualization

Dear Friend,

Some people say that they cannot visualize or image. With practice most of us can learn to visualize and image and help bring about good we want in our lives. Today we start to exercise our visualization power, for we all have it.

Let us think about a trip we want to take. We want a good trip so we think words like happy, safe, successful, orderly, prosperous, comfortable, blessed. With your eyes closed you can see the words. If you can't tell yourself to see them, it will help if you mentally draw the letters or the words that describe the kind of trip you want. Or you have a meeting, perhaps an interview. See yourself in the clothes you will wear. See yourself getting into the car, bus or plane. See the place where you will go for the meeting. See the people. Image the interviewer sitting down but getting up to greet you with a smile, and, with outstretched hand to shake your hand and then motioning you to sit down. See yourself, feel yourself easy in the interview, picture the successful outcome.

Even if there is no immediate trip or interview in your life, try these today. It is good practice and you can visualize desired good and help it come.

## Enjoying Us

Dear Friend,

Today we are going to enjoy being us. We are going to enjoy ourselves. If we have been hurting, sad, depressed, angry, resentful, feeling guilty, we stop that for today.

Today we enjoy ourselves and we certainly can't enjoy a sad, depressed, angry person. If we were someone else who was sad, depressed, angry, we'd stay clear of us. We stay clear of that part of us today. We think only of the nice parts of us, the happy parts.

We think about our wonderful bodies, our marvelous emotional nature that can respond to others and to things, think about our wonderful minds that can decide good things for us and picture more good for us. We think about the kind things we have done and plan to do, we think about the capacity to love that is in us, we think about every good thing there is about us and we may be surprised to find the good that is in us. There is so much for you and me to enjoy in us.

Too often we think only of enjoying others but in our personal world we are all that is there and we need to be happy in this world of our own and find enjoyment. There is a way to be happy with us there. What we are really doing is finding God in us, finding the good God created in us, finding our God Self. Today we enjoy ourselves and, as we do, we will be much more enjoyable to others.

## Thanks For Us

Dear Friend,

   Let us give thanks. Let us give thanks for special things and for things we have taken for granted, things we are so used to having that we do not think about them as needing to be thanked.

   Take our minds, our emotions and bodies. How recently have we thanked them for the wonder they are? We couldn't operate without them. They are so wonderfully created that they not only make life possible but make it possible to make our lives what we want them to be. Our minds take care of all our activity, give us ideas, make it possible for us to succeed. There is no limit to our minds. Our bodies have been created so that they can maintain vitality even if we are not good to them. Have we thanked our bodies for their work for us, for their ability to heal, adjust and renew? Have we thanked our emotional nature recently? Life would be very dull if we did not have this part of us. Gone would be all feeling. Gone would be joy and laughter, gone would be appreciation, gone would be delight and love. Life would be dull. Today we appreciate all of us. We give thanks for our fantastically created bodies and for our unlimitedly potential minds. We give thanks for life itself and for our life.

   God has created us wonderfully and we are grateful today and we express that gratitude.

## We Can Change

Dear Friend,

Today we are going to think about the greatest discovery we can make, a discovery that can make us all we want to be and have all we need to have, do all we desire to do. That discovery is not a recent one, but it is always new because each of us has to discover it for himself.

That discovery is that we can change our lives, change conditions, change ourselves by changing the way we are thinking, change our thoughts and our emotions, change the way we say things. It is the discovery of the power we were created with, the power to create our experiences, our potential. It's a priceless discovery.

We can change ourselves, we can change what is happening to us. We can change what we are doing.

Sometimes we make this discovery but we don't use it. Today we look at our lives. Are we happy with them? Is there anything we would like changed? Most of us will find there is and we are ready to change and we pray, "Father-Mother God, thank You for Your help in my changing my thinking in areas of my life that need to be different. I want to change certain things. I want to change the way I think and feel about them." God will help us make the change. God wants our lives wonderful. They can be.

## I Am a Divine Idea

Dear Friend,

"I am a divine idea in the Mind of God." We can read the words, we can hear the words, we can say the words but until we accept them we may have a question to ask ourselves: Am I really a divine idea in the Mind of God? Can I really believe that I am a divine idea? Can I think that in the Mind of God I am?

We say the words first with question, then we can take a deep breath and say them with wonder, "I am a divine idea in the Mind of God." There has to be blending of God and us for we are here. We think of the everywhereness of God's Mind. We know that there has to be a blending, a oneness, for we, our minds, our bodies, all of us are part of the allness of God, part of the everywhereness of God. We think of all the people we know, of all people everywhere. Everyone is a divine idea in the Mind of God!

We try to grasp the magnitude of this knowing. The wonder of it is thought stopping. We're more important to the universe than we realized. It's true. We know too, that God provides for all God Ideas so we will have all that is needed for our special expression, our special expression as the special divine idea we are.

We think about expressing God today in all of our activities and it is a wonderful day.

## Do-It-Ourself Life

Dear Friend,

There are many self-help books. There are many articles, that tell us how to "do it" ourself. Our life is really a do-it-ourself life. As a newborn, we have to take the breath of life ourself, before we can live. We have to be able to take nourishment. We have to adjust to the change in our environment, the change from our mother's body to the world where we are in so many ways on our own. As we grow we have to take first steps, say first words, we have to learn to read, to write, to multiply. Whether or not we are a success, happy and healthy is largely up to us.

Whether or not we are happy may seem to depend on others, but we are learning it doesn't. It is ours to do. It is up to us to do what needs to be done for our prosperity and our health. It's wonderful that we have a do-it-ourself life. How awful it would be if we had to depend on others to do everything for us, if we were at the direction of others, if our health, our joy, our success depended on others.

Today we sing thanks and praise to our Father-Mother God for making us do-it-ourselves people, with making it possible for us to do and to have and to be whatever we desire and act to bring about. We know God will help us. But we do it! We start, God helps. How wonderful! Our possibilities are unlimited, and we can make use of them now.

## I Do My Part

Dear Friend,

God action can be in our world adjusting, cleansing, purifying, healing, harmonizing, prospering. Right activity is never all on God's part. We have a part to do. God is not to do for us what we can do for ourselves.

It's a little like exercise. Exercise does great things for us. We have nothing to do with results of exercise but we have to exercise. That's our part. It's the same with getting rid of unwanted habits. We have our part to do. We can't reach for a cigarette and at the same time affirm that God is taking away our desire for a smoke. We can't allow anger to surge up in us and affirm God is bringing us peace. There is always something for us to do. In us is the divinity that is always gravitating toward greater good.

In us there is this wonderful something that is waiting to assist us toward peace, joy, success, health and wholeness. Today we do our part. Even if we don't know now what that part is, we pray, and God lets us know.

We say many times today, "I am doing my part. I am making it possible for God help to be done for me and through me. I am doing my part to make it possible for God action to take place in my life now."

## Onnnnn Our Way

Dear Friend,

Many of us have heard, read or made OM sound in meditation groups or by ourselves. It is said to be the oldest meditative sound. It is said to open us up to new spiritual understanding and new spiritual experience. It is an UP experience. It is an ON experience. It is a tone prayer. It has helped people make spiritual progress. Often we come to a place where, "the world is too much with us," but we know we must go on.

Thinking about this, the idea came to me that perhaps that is what the "ommmmm" is, really the "onnnnn" signal. The "m" and the "n" are close in sound. Their vibrations are similar. We can sound the "onnnnn" sound as well as the "ommmmm" when we need something to spur us on, to get us going again. We can make this an on going day. If we have any feeling of depression we know that it is going to go as we say "onnnnn, onnnnn, onnnnn." And we will be *on* our way to happiness, love, health, joy, strength, healing, success, prosperity right now.

We are onnnnn our way to spiritual understanding, onnnnn to whatever we need, whatever we desire. We are onnnnn our way. This is our musical prayer.

## Place to Start

Dear Friend,

Sometimes we think that before we can be better in any way or before we can have things we want, before we can have circumstances the way we want them, we have to do a lot of things, have a lot of understanding, have people help us. Oh, we can think of so many things we feel we have to have before there can be changes for good in our lives. This is not so. We only have to start where we are with what we have and with what we are. Nothing else.

We start now and we stop putting it off into the distant future. With whatever we have, we start. We do not start alone. We start with God's help, knowing God will help us all the way. God will direct us to what we need next, what we need to do next. God will provide opportunities for us. The important thing is to start, so we do. We start with God. We look around to see what there is for us to do about what we want. There is always something. This is the real beginning. We do this, we take care of that, we expect to know what next to do. We stay with God. We have an excited feeling. We are beginning. We are on our way, on our way to whatever good we need and we give thanks that whatever our beginning is, God is with us to support us. We are not alone. We cannot be alone when we start where we are knowing where we want to go with God's help.

## It's a New Day

Dear Friend,

Today is a new day. We wipe the blackboard of what is past. Today's blackboard is clean and we write on it what we want today to be. If there is any kind of confusion in our lives, now is the time to look at our lives and know that order can be in every part of our life. Order brings newness. Order brings progress. We start with the immediate, with what should be done today or with something that is bothering us the most. We think about this part of our lives and, if it is something we can look at physically, we sit and look at or stand and look at it and we say lovingly and firmly, "Divine Order is now established in you and Divine Order will be maintained in you. God is helping me get Divine Order going in you now and I give thanks that Order is here now."

Then we close our eyes for a moment and visualize the situation or condition as it will be when order is there. We tell ourselves that order can come no matter how impossible it may appear. We remind ourselves that God created an orderly universe and as God's children we too can create an orderly world of our own. We will know what to do. God in us will tell us. We will have the strength and energy and determination necessary to do what has to be done. We keep the vision of order in our minds as we no longer hesitate to get order started and we continuously give thanks today for new order in our lives and order comes and it is a wonderful new day, a wonderful new day God has given us to make orderly and we thank God all day long.

## Our Wants

Dear Friend,

Let's think about what we want. We can have so many wants. We often say that we want this and we want that, we want to do this, we want to do that. Do we really want what we say we want? Will we be able to take care of and handle what we say we want? Do we want it now? Is it something really good for us to have? We need to be careful what we say we want to do and have.

Maybe it is "Oh, I want to get married." Are we ready for marriage? Maybe we want an expensive, beautiful car. Do we have a place to keep it, are we going to be able to pay for it and maintain it easily? If a trip to Europe were possible, would we be able to get off from work? Would there be someone to take care of our other responsibilities? Or a million dollars, would we be ready for a million dollars? We can laugh and say, "Oh, of course, who couldn't take care of a million dollars?" but there would be all kinds of decisions to make, much to learn and learn quickly about handling a million. Yes, we could spend it but most of us think that with a million we would be taken care of from now on. We would not be if we didn't know how to handle it. Today let's think about our wants and objectively decide, "Are we ready for them?" If not and we really want them, then we get ready for them. God will help us choose and God will help us get ready.

## Wonderful Promise

Dear Friend,

There is such a wonderful promise in the Bible. In the first Psalm is a promise that everything we do will prosper. Everything we do will come out right. Everything we do will bring the kind of results that we want. Oh, yes, there is something we are to do. There always is. Everyone of the wonderful promises in the Bible has something for us to do, perhaps to believe, perhaps to seek, perhaps to delight in the Lord.

In this one it is a special blessing promise for everyone who stays with righteousness, who lives as rightly as he can, who doesn't judge others, who doesn't do things he knows are not right, who stays close to God and knows God's laws and promises. It's a big promise.

God is never small. Everything, everything we do will be successful, prosper, be good. It cannot help coming that way when we stay close to God, when we let God direct our way and do not depend on others or do not condemn or judge others. This is not impossible. We pray and and we pray often, "Father-Mother God, I want to walk with You, I want You to direct everything I do. I want to be non-critical. I want to see good, You, in all people and all happenings. I want to do only things that are good. I know You will help me and I know that with Your help everything I do will prosper, will turn out good, be successful, and I give thanks right now and all the time."

## Competition Not Needed

Dear Friend,

We can get out of the competition game because we do not have to compete. We are individually created and actually can not compete and have no need to compete. With our individual differences, individual talents and skills, we need only develop them and become the best possible us that we can. We then let the special divine plan we have unfold.

One way to help ourselves is to know that in every transaction, we must be sure both sides gain. We must strive to always give more than comes back to us in actual gain. We want to give that extra that is not required, not called for, doesn't have to be given. Much can then come back to us. Anytime we are in a situation where one side is going to lose, we should get out of it, or give in some way extra good to the other party so that there is gain and not loss. Whenever we are dealing with others we keep in our minds and hearts, "Everyone in this matter is going to gain, no one is going to lose," and we ask our Father-Mother God to help us bring that about. It is always possible.

It is a giving and, when we want to give, there is always something to give and then there is always more to receive. We have everything to gain when we see to it that everyone involved gains in every transaction we are part of. What a good feeling this brings us, brings everyone in the situation and we can have it this way with God's help and God will give it every time.

We do not compete, we develop our talents and we give.

## Supply and Supplier

Dear Friend,

All day we think of God as our supply and our supplier. God is both. God is the one and only supplier and the one and only Source of supply. Life gets simplified when we accept this and live with it. When we need healing we turn to God, Source of life, Source of healing, Source of strength and energy, Source of wisdom in telling us what we are to do about our physical condition. We need a job. We turn first to God knowing that God is our employer and knows where we are to work. We turn to God, having faith that God will direct us to the special job God wants us to have. We follow intuition.

We listen. We heed suggestions and ideas that come. We need money. We turn first to God knowing that God is the Source of all good and all good includes money. God is the Supply and God the Supplier. Usually, our supply comes through our following God ideas of what to do about our financial situation once we have turned to God. We want love se we turn to God Who is love and loves us. God ideas will come that will start us expressing love more and attracting love to us.

We want happiness. We don't waste time wish-thinking that happiness would be ours if certain people did certain things or if we met certain people. We turn to God knowing that God ideas will help us attract happiness and will help us in our endeavor to be happy. Our happiness is up to us. God will bring us happy opportunities. We go first to God for any need because God is the one and only Supply and Supplier.

## Abundance Is Ours

Dear Friend,

Today we expect the more abundant life, more abundant in every good way. Abundance is to be ours because we are the rich children of God. We think about the wonder of abundance, think about abundance and what it means and then immediately think abundance as ours. Abundance coming, abundance that already has our names on it.

It's heady stuff to think about because abundance of all good has everything we can ever desire in it: health, happiness, peace of mind, happy relationships, strength, wisdom, guidance, money, things, time to enjoy all of the good we are bringing to us. It's good we think about this as being heady stuff for it is in the head, in the mind, that our abundance begins. We keep out of our conscious thinking any thought of lack, any thought of depletion or limitation. We fill our minds and hearts and keep them filled with thoughts and feelings of richness, of abundance, of rich and lavish supply of all we can need or desire. We feel that not only is abundance possible but it is possible for us. It is sure.

The blessings of the Lord are sure and God only thinks and does in rich and wonderful ways. He told Abraham he could have all he could see. We can have all that we can anticipate, all that we can envision as ours, all that we can richly feel is for us. We give thanks for God's rich abundance for us and for all the world. We are all God's rich children who can have an abundance of every good thing.

## Graduation Not Failure

Dear Friend,

Have you failed anything or anyone? If you have, and most of us have, that failure stays with us and we keep feeling the special misery failure brings. Let's look at our failure or our failures as graduations. No matter how serious we think the failure was we learned a lot. We tried a lot. We didn't want to fail. We wanted to succeed.

We recognize the trying, the desire, the work, the learning and know that it was an education, not a failure and we have graduated from whatever it was. The graduation may let us feel that we can start into another school, activity or project using what we have learned, using the growth we made. We don't pull back from a new job that appears to be the same as one we failed. We won't be afraid of a new relationship, of any new responsibility we have not yet handled successfully.

We go into new activities happily expecting success, not wondering if we are going to fail. We take with us to the new only the desire to succeed, the desire to enjoy the new activity and the added strength we have from all the learning and all the experiencing we have had in the past. We have not failed, we have graduated, graduated to success.

# Confidence Injection

Dear Friend,

Sometimes we need an injection of confidence. Sometimes we find ourselves as a man told me one time, "all run out of confidence." We may be called upon to do things we don't really know how to do, we may be expected to do things we don't see how we can. We may be facing situations we have had no preparation to face. Oh, so many times we can feel a lack of confidence. Always we have a choice: to pick up our confidence, give up or go on scared.

What we really want is confidence. The beauty and the wonder is that there is unlimited confidence for us because within us there is unlimited knowing how, unlimited strength, unlimited courage, unlimited ability to do whatever is ours to do. That strength, courage and ability to do whatever is ours to do. That strength, courage and ability is the God strength, God courage, God ability, God knowing that is always in us because God is in us, all of God. We can say, "I am confident because God in me is confident."

In the Bible, God is compared to a buckler, a tower of strength, a rock. This is for us today. God is our armor for the day. When we remember God in us, we are putting on our armor. We are giving ourselves a tower of strength. That's all we need. It does not matter how lacking in confidence we have been, today we can be confident. God is our confidence. As we affirm this we will believe that we can do what we have to do. We can!

### Are We Ready?

Dear Friend,

We all want to have increase of good in our lives. We want increase of health and strength, we want increase of joy and happiness, money, of success, but are we sure we are ready for increase? Are we ready to do the things that will bring us greater health and strength? Are we ready to choose right foods, exercise regularly, get sufficient rest? Are we ready to not let anything make us unhappy? Are we ready to study, think of better ways to do our work, improve our personality, be better, more efficient in every way so that we can have increase of success? Are we taking care of the money we have, are we blessing it, remembering our money as all of our good comes from God, are we using wisdom in the use of money we now have? If so, then we are getting ready for increase of every kind.

Do we really want increase or are we just saying the words? Do we want more good, more understanding of ourselves and others, of God? Are we willing to study, pray, meditate, think? There is always much for us to do to be ready for increase of good. Happily we don't have to do it alone. God is with us to help and direct us to get ready and then help bring new good to us.

## Hoarding Doesn't Pay

Dear Friend,

I do not hold back, I do not hoard, I do not withhold good from others. I share. I try to help others in every possible way. I want others to prosper, to have good things happen to them. I am glad when good things happen to others. I do not feel anyone's good is a threat to me. I do not think that I should have what they have. I know God's good for me is unlimited. I know that there is unlimited good for me.

I know if I hoard and hang on to things they spoil. I know that if I don't give and don't try to help others attain their good I am cutting myself off from the pleasure of giving and I know too that I am cutting myself off from the receiving that always come through giving.

Whenever I withhold good of any kind from anyone I am cutting off my good in some way. I will have good in some part of my life withheld from me. Not as punishment but because I have put the law of cause and effect into action. It is as we give that we receive and if we give with withholding or, if we give with reluctance that withholding or reluctance is coming back to us.

So we pray, "Father-Mother God, help me not hold back other's good, help me not hoard. I want prosperity for others, success, happiness, health, good of every kind." We cannot lose when we give. Today we want to give and we do.

## Give to Live

Dear Friend,

Rhymes come to us at odd times. I awakened one night and heard these words repeated over and over, "Give, give, give and really live." We have to give before we can live fully. I like jingles. I like rhymes. The words stayed with me. We all have so much to give whether we think we do or not.

When we smile, we give happiness out to the world. When we tell someone something nice and true about them, we give that person a wonderful gift, a gift that can help him like himself better.

We can give other people a lift, we can give money, we can give time, we can give love.

There is so much that we can give today, right now. You and I often have little urges inside us that say, "Give that person this . . . ." Perhaps it is a phone call, perhaps it is a thank you, perhaps it is a suggestion.

All of life is geared to giving. The sun gives heat and light, rain is given us, the grass, plants, trees give us beauty and food. The night gives time for rest and renewal. We can give our Father-Mother God our attention, our devotion, our appreciation, give our prayers and meditations. We have so much to give and today we give. We remember, "Give, give, give and really live."

Today we give and really live.

## Radiating Love

Dear Friend,

"I am a radiating center of Divine Love mighty to attract my good and radiate good to others." We've heard this, we've read it, we've thought about it but do we actually believe it? It's quite a thing to think about ourselves as a radiating center of Divine Love. Let's picture this radiating center *in* us.

We may see it as spokes going around and around as on a wheel. We may see lights circling. We may see colors swirling. We may feel an energy that goes and goes and goes. We may feel a warmth that seems to go all through us and out. This is one thing we notice, *everything goes out*.

There is something in us that radiates, that moves, that energizes, and that goes out. This is love, God's love, Divine Love. It is in us all the time. It is waiting to be allowed to circle, to spin, to accelerate in energy, to go out to bless the world. We let it go out and we let love come back in. The energy we feel begins the outflow so that there can be inflow. When we feel it, we are beginning to realize our radiating center, our love center. Love radiates only good and attracts only good.

We say and feel the words, "I am a radiating center of Divine Love, mighty to attract good and mighty to radiate good to others." We say it many times today and we feel our radiation, we feel love going out and we know love will come back to us.

## True Giving

Dear Friend,

Let's think about giving. We are likely to think more about gifts than giving and there is a difference. Gifts should be the outcome of giving. Gifts themselves are not the giving. Giving begins with the desire to give. Giving should continue with that desire saturated with love and wisdom. When we start with love and wisdom, ideas come that are right. The gift will be right in every way. If we think gifts with dollar signs between us and seeing the right gift, we've lost our givingness. When we put the giving with love first, ideas come that take care of the dollar signs. Love works.

Love works miracles in every way. Love works miracles in gift ideas, gift buying and selecting. Love takes all negativity out of giving. Love makes giving a joy and not an obligation. Love brings the right things to the right person in the right way and at the right price. Today we give thanks for our Father-Mother's help in giving, in giving with love and we pray, "Father-Mother God, thank You for helping me think giving not gifts. When I do, I know gifts will come naturally and perfectly."

Today we give, we feel givingness, we feel the joy of giving and gifts come easily. We give first through our minds and hearts. Then love, God, takes care of the giving.

## Good Discontent

Dear Friend,

Let's think about discontent today. Often we are discontented. We can be discontented with our jobs, with our homes, with our daily routine and we can be discontented with ourselves. Discontent is not necessarily bad.

Discontent can spur us on to better situations and conditions. Without discontent, improvements would not be made. Without discontent in the minds and hearts of inventors, new good ways of doing things would never be invented. Discontent with world problems will bring solutions, improvements. In our own lives we need divine discontent so that we will reach for greater spiritual understanding and experience.

Discontent, however, has another side to it. There's always the constructive and destructive, the positive and negative, the plus and minus. We can let discontent lead us to despondency, to wringing our hands and beating our breasts. We can let discontent make us complaining, critical, deciding that there is nothing we can do about things, discontented. It can make our faces unattractive because discontent shows on our faces. It can affect the way we stand and walk and how we talk. We can let discontent keep us from doing good work, keep us from expecting the good that is ours. Today we look at any discontent we have, and we see how we are handling it. We ask God's help in making our discontent become the push for new good. It can be and it will be.

## We Can

Dear Friend,

Today let's you and I do something that we have been doing our best to avoid doing. Something we may have tucked back telling ourselves we would get to it but not wanting to do it, perhaps because we didn't feel we could do a good job of it. We may not feel equal to it. We may feel we don't have the energy to do it. We may question our mental ability. We may feel that we do not have time to do it. It does not matter why we are not getting it done. Today we do it.

We remember the wonderful words of Paul in Phillipians, "I can do all things through Christ which strengthens me." The Christ in us, the divine part of us, the spiritual part of us, God in us can do it. We remember how Jesus the Christ disclaimed credit for what He had accomplished by saying it was not He who had done wonderful things, not He who had performed miracles but the Father in Him.

Today we can let the Father in us help us get done what we have not been doing and what has become a burden to us because we have not done it. All things are possible for us to accomplish if we let God help us. We use the wonderful prayer statement many times, "All things I am, can do and be through the Christ that is in me." All things. We can be all we need to be, do all we need to do. We are capable today. We give thanks that we are.

70

## Day of Miracles

Dear Friend,

Today we think about miracles. Isn't it a happy thing to think about? We baptize today our Day of Miracles and it will be. Does this mean that we expect to have supernatural things happen? Do we expect natural laws to be set aside? Too often we think about miracles in this way.

Miracles get things to the way they should be. The miracle of healing brings us to our natural state of health and wholeness. The miracle of a job gets us to the place where we should be, doing constructive, productive work. The miracle of joy brings us back to the place where we were created to be, a joy filled child of God. The miracle of peace and harmony merely restores us, a group, a business, a nation to where we should be in tune with the harmony of the universe.

Miracles start in our minds, miracles start with our remembering that we are the sons and daughters of our rich, all loving, all wise, all caring Father-Mother God. Miracles start with our knowing miracles are possible. Miracles start with our expecting whatever lack or problem we have to be solved, to have our lives as they should be. Miracles start with thought, then comes the feeling that miracles are about to happen. When we get that feeling we are ready to know with all our being that miracles are happening.

Today is our day for miracles to happen, for things to get right. God helps when we start miracles happening. We give thanks for the wonder and the possibility of miracles.

## Health-Filled Day

Dear Friend,

Today we give thanks for perfect health, for bound-less strength, for vim and vigor. Even if we are not well, even if we have not been well for sometime, today we feel health returning, strength returning. We feel our bodies reacting in healthy ways. We remember the healing power that is in us all the time. We concentrate on it, we do not focus on hurts or symptoms or on what we've been told. We tell ourselves health truths today.

We tell our bodies they are so wonderful and blessed, blessed with this healing, renewing, restoring power. We tell our bodies, "This is the day that the Lord has made for you to feel wonderful, strong, vigorous, well and whole." We thank the Father-Mother God of us that we have been created this way. We give thanks for our minds that can direct our bodies toward health and healing. We give thanks for our responsive bodies, thanks for every wonderful, intelligent cell that knows its own wonderfulness and, with our encouragement and appreciation, will speedily do its own special work.

We think health. We think strength. We think vim and vigor. We are enthusiastic about the feeling of health that is starting to go full tilt in us. This is a wonderful day. It is a day of health, wonderful boundless health, and we give thanks for every second of this health-filled day.

## Happy Day of Love

Dear Friend,

Let's have an especially happy day by making this a day of love. Oh, I am sure you and I have already been loving to someone today but let's see how much more love we can give out today. We will give love out without any thought of love's coming back to us in any certain way. There will be people we will feel free to tell, "I love you." There will be others that we will think "I love you," as we smile at them. There will be others that we will do something for and, while we do, we will think and feel, "I love you."

Wherever we are and whatever we are doing today, we love. We think lovingly of everyone. We think lovingly and do loving things for people we haven't been loving. We reach out to more people to love and express love to. As we love today we will be loving our Father-Mother God more than ever because God is love and all love is of God. When we love we are more God like and when we love we are expressing the God in us more definitely, more beautifully.

We will find that everything we have to do today will be easily and quickly done. We are likely to make new friends today. People we have not liked very well or with whom we have been on bad terms will seem to change. Love changes people, love changes situations and circumstances. Today we love and we will find that today is full of love. It is a day of love. How happy today will be. How wonderful!

## Day of Blessing

Dear Friend,

Today you and I are going to make this a day of blessing others. Today we deliberately think first of others and of good we want them to have. When something occurs, Let's think "Oh, bless you," rather than "Why did you do that?" or "That was stupid." We'll bless those we might otherwise feel a bit of envy about. We'll bless those we let overpower us. We'll bless those who may make excessive demands of us. The moment we bless others, we have blessed ourselves and we change.

We calm, we cool, we relax. This makes it easier for us to think clearly, much easier to do and say the right thing. Today we bless everyone we are around, everyone we see even at a distance, everyone we think about. We start right now. We give thanks to our Father-Mother God for the power to bless, for the magic of blessing, for the wonder of letting loose good for others, for helping others enjoy the good that is for them. And we pray, "Father-Mother God, help me not forget anyone today. Help me remember everyone today with a blessing. Help me think blessings, help me say blessings, help me feel blessings. Thank You." Every day has its specialness. Today will have the specialness of giving generously of our blessings and we will be blessed. What we give always comes back to us.

# Grab Day

Dear Friend,

Today is our Grab Day. Our day to grab our good, our day to grab back our good. If we are feeling lost, feeling lack, feeling unloved, feeling angry or sad let's make a grab. Let's grab for direction, for knowing where we are and how to go. Let's grab for plenty, let's grab for love. Let's grab for peace and calm, let's grab for happiness and complete joy.

If we find that we are thinking negative thoughts of any kind, let's grab for positive ones. If we've been thinking lack or sickness and unhappiness, let's grab back the way we want to think. Let's grab for affirmations that will remind us that we are the children of a loving, all providing, caring Father-Mother. We remind ourselves that we are to have all good and that includes sufficient money, sufficient strength, health and plenty of joy.

We stop any negative thinking and grab for an opposite. Sometimes we find ourselves reaching out blindly but that positive affirmation, that positive prayer is within reach. We can reach it. We can grab it. We can use it and we can make it ours. And, when we grab for good, good comes and stays because when we grab any thing we hang on to it. When we grab for something, we have to let something go. What we're letting go today we don't want, and we don't want any more of it. We're grabbing for what we want and it is good.

## A Fun Day

Dear Friend,

Today we're going to have fun. We're going to declare our perfection. This is going to be a happy day. Let's make it a game. If we get straight faced and serious about this, we will start thinking, "Oh, I can't be perfect." We remember that Jesus the Christ told us we were to be perfect. Playing this game today can get us started toward that perfection. It can open us up to possibility.

We want no limits today. We want perfection. To help us think and accept the possibility of our becoming perfect, we're going to give our day the fun touch. We start right now, no matter how far from perfection we now are. We start with complete perfection.

We declare: "I am God's perfect child. Yes, I am. I am God's rich and successful child. Yes, I am. I am God's happy child. Yes, I am. I am my perfect age. Yes, I am. I am God's perfectly wise and understanding child. Yes, I am. I am enjoying perfect health. Yes, I am. I am strong. I am vigorous, I am filled with energy and vim. Yes, I am. I am God's beautiful, handsome child, Yes, I am."

Whatever we don't think we are or don't have, today we declare we have and we are.

Don't you feel better already about yourself? I do. Don't you feel happier? I do. This is our perfect day. This is our fun day, our happy day. This is the day we de-limit us. Perfection is possible and we're finding perfection can be fun.

"Today I have fun knowing my perfection."

76

### Grace Is Love

Dear Friend,

Grace is a difficult concept for many of us. We can think of grace as the love of God. Grace means favorably disposed toward someone and that is what love does. It means giving mercy or pardon, it means to be in someone's good feelings about us. All this is love. Because grace is God's love it is for everyone. It does not depend on any acceptance of any creed. All people are equal in the eyes and love of God.

God always is ready as love is to come toward us, to meet us and to meet us any place. Love, God's love, is for us everywhere no matter what we have done or not done. God's love meets us with open arms as we turn toward God.

It is through grace, through love, that we know that we are forgiven and it is our giving grace, giving love to others, that makes it possible for us to forgive others. It is through grace, through love, that we find healing for our mind, emotions, body, and circumstances.

We feel so much better about everything in our lives today as we think of grace as love and know that it is for us and we can say jubilantly, "Through the grace of God I am forgiven and healed," and we will be.

## Don't Stew

Dear Friend,

So often we get in an uproar about things, we allow ourselves to get in turmoil and then we are not able to think clearly. Today let's not stew. Today when we feel that we are getting upset, let's tell ourselves, "Don't stew. Don't stew." We say it as more than a suggestion, we say it as a firm directive, a command.

Our mind will hear, both our conscious mind and our subconscious minds will hear, and quiet will come. Often we are like a pan left on the heat longer than it should be and the contents boil over. We can boil over in anger, in impatience, in fear. We always get a signal from the pan that it is about to boil over. Our bodies and emotions, our minds tell us when we are about to boil over.

Sometimes we don't respond to the pan's signal, sometimes we don't respond to our signal. We can watch, we can be aware and we can turn our heat down. It is turning down when we say to ourselves, "Don't stew, quit stewing." God will help us for this directive to ourselves is really a prayer. It is an expressed desire for peace and calm. We can pray, "God, help me not stew. Help me not boil over." And God will and we say "Thank You, thank You, Father-Mother God, for the calm and the peace that is coming to me now. With Your help I can take care of everything peacefully."

## Gift of 'Thank You'

Dear Friend,

We can forget to say "thank you." We can be so happy with what we have been told or given, so very excited that someone has done something for us that we actually don't think to say the words. We may feel them intensely within us but we do have to say them so that others will not have even an instant's unsureness of our appreciation for what they have done or given us. Not that they have done it for thanks but they need to know they are appreciated. And we need to express out loud our gratitude.

It does something good for us when we say "thank you." It diminishes our good when we are neglectful. It is more than courtesy. It is more than good manners. It is the giving that we can give in return for what we have received. The gift or the service is incomplete without the thanks. We increase the value of the gift with our saying "thank you." Why else would there be more than one reminder in the Bible that we were to rejoice and give thanks?

Rejoice and give thanks. We do rejoice when we are given. That is the first part. The second and completing part is to give thanks. Even if our rejoicing is such that we jump up and down we are so happy, we remember today that we are going to add that completer. We will give thanks. We will rejoice and give thanks and give that gift to the giver.

79

## Healing Is Now

Dear Friend,

When there is a need for healing, we start quickly remembering that healing is possible, that healing has already started. Healing is going on before the flow of blood stops, before the pain stops, while the fever rages. No matter what conditions are, all that matters is that we turn at once to healing. Turn away from pain, turn away from bleeding, from fever, turn away from what anyone is saying about our condition.

Healing, healing, healing, there is healing. There is healing power. We bless our bodies. We bless whoever is helping us. God works through all of them. We decree that each one is letting God's wisdom and love and understanding, God's creative power work through them. It is not necessary that they know that it is God in them that is telling them what to do, guiding every move they make, every decision.

It is God's caring for us. We can trust God. We can relax, release all concern to God and accept healing, accept all healing help. In our minds, in our hearts, all through our bodies we feel healing, healing, healing now. Today there is healing, Right now there is healing and we give thanks that this is so.

# Pain Goes

Deqr Friend,

There are many kinds of pain. Thoughts can be painful. Memories. We can have physical pain. No one wants pain of any kind. Pain always comes with tension, whether that tension is mental or physical. When we realize this, our first action will be to relax. Relax anxious expectation of continuing pain or increasing pain, relax all our body.

We go through our body, relaxing each area. Then we look away from the pain. We affirm our freedom from pain. And, we give thanks for the pain. Pain is a wonderful help. It tells us that something is wrong. As we relax, we will let knowing what is causing the pain come through to us so that we can do something about the cause. When we do, pain, the effect of that cause, can be handled.

Often the relaxation and the turning to the cause and not the pain eradicates the pain at once. Sometimes it takes a denial of pain's hold on us and an affirming of God's healing love at work in our minds, bodies and emotions. We pray now, "Father-Mother God, thank You for helping me know what I can do to get rid of the cause. I give this pain to You for Your loving elimination." We relax, we give to God, we listen and do. Pain goes.

## Regeneration

Dear Friend,

Today we think about the renewal of our bodies, re-generation. Our bodies are renewed, as Paul tells us, by the renewal of our minds. When we change our thinking about life, about our bodies, our bodies respond.

Whenever we allow ourselves to be unhappy or angry or guilty we put a heavy load on the cells of our bodies. When we look at life with expectation of happy, rich good, then we free our body cells to do all they have been created to do and to be. Eternal youth is a God idea.

People grow old because they expect to grow old and because they accept all that our culture thinks about aging. Our cells were not created to wear out. Our bodies are fantastically able to renew. Take our hands. Scientists tell us that no known metal could take what our hands take during a year and not be worn thin. We know our bodies recuperate after illness, after fatigue. We are told in Isaiah that our strength can be renewed and that we can run and not walk and we can do and not tire.

Today we tell ourselves this and we will feel and see the difference. Others will too. We will not talk about getting older, neither will we talk about anyone's getting older. We will not talk about any lack of strength or energy. We will feel our bodies respond to our changed way of thinking. We will be renewed.

## Love Revives

Dear Friend,

Today we are going to center our love on something in our life that appears to be sick or dying. Perhaps it will be someone who is not well and we will give healing love to that person. We will feel love healing, cleansing, purifying, strengthening that person. It may be a sick relationship. We will pour our love into that relationship, not thinking that the love is going to work in any certain way or that anyone is going to do any certain things but we will pour love into that relationship knowing that love can do the miraculous.

Love can make all things right. It may be our finances that need love. Finances respond to love as they respond to thoughts of lack and fear. Today we love our money.

Perhaps it is ourselves that need healing love. Today we give love and understanding to us. We love the specialness of us, we love the truth that we are a son or daughter of an all loving-providing, caring, supporting Father-Mother God. We love all our possibilities. We love all that has been in our lives, the so-called good and the so-called ungood—all of it has brought us where we are and we are prepared for a wonderful today and tomorrow. We love the divinity in us, that part of God that is us, that part of us that expresses God as us. Today we love ourselves and we love others. It is a day of reviving, healing love and we expect new life in our world.

## Enough Time

Dear Friend,

Today we have time for everything that we need to do. We are not going to worry about what we are going to get done. We simply do first one thing and then another and we're going to enjoy every moment of this day. We cannot enjoy anything, we cannot do our best when we are concerned about things that are ahead to do. We concentrate on this moment, right now.

What I am doing now is all I need to think about. I give this moment my complete attention and what I am doing now gets done as it should. Then I pick up the next and then the next. I take time to relax between jobs. It may be for only a moment. But I let everything go and turn within to my Father-Mother God who is never tired, never in a hurry, always knows what to do next and how to do it. This God in me who can tell me when I am doing things wrong or when I am doing things I don't really have to do. This God in me that is my strength, my wisdom, my energy, my enthusiasm, my love, my joy, my ability.

I give thanks for God in me that can do all things and can help me do all the things that I need to do today. God in me is my all. God in me helps me get everything done today and gives me time to enjoy what I am doing and enjoy people and things around me.

We do not have to face today alone. We have help. God helps us do it all, all that we have to do today.

## Change of Pace

Dear Friend,

Let's think about change of pace today. Jesus the Christ did this. After He had been with the crowds, after He had talked and healed and loved and listened and cared for people He would go away. He would go out to sea in a boat, or He would go to a mountain. We need to do this.

We can become aware that we are going too fast, we are trying to do too much. Then we need to tell ourselves that we have done plenty for right now. We change our pace. We slow down. We go where we can slow down. It may be that we will only go from a very busy, fast moving job to a slower, less hurrying kind of work. It may be to do something quite different. We may go for a walk. We may go to a window and look out to a new view. No matter what the view is, our back is turned from our busyness. We deliberately change our pace.

We know metaphysically that water is calming, understanding, cleansing and to go to the mountains means to raise our consciousness, to pray, to meditate, to become still in mind and heart and body. When we do these things we let go of hurry, of pressure. We get new strength, new vitality. We become new. Today we change our pace whenever it is necessary. We think of Jesus the Christ, always our Way Shower. He changed His pace. He slowed down. He refilled. He left the hubub for the quiet. So can we. Today we do.

## Enjoy Aloneness

Dear Friend,

Today you and I are going to enjoy aloneness. No, not loneliness. There is a difference between being alone and being lonely. We need time alone. We need time to relax our bodies and our minds, a time of quiet when we can catch up with ourselves, a time when there are no people demands on our attention. We need a time to regain emotional balance, to get a new perspective of work and relationships. A time to sort our feelings, our goals. A time to plan.

Sometimes we are afraid to be alone. It may be that we are afraid that we will miss something if we do not stay with people. It may be that we are not on good terms with ourselves. We will never get to be friends with us if we are always with people. We will never have the opportunity to really know who we are and what we are thinking and feeling. We won't know what we really want to do. If we don't have alone time, we will miss out on us and this is most important for our present and our future.

No matter how busy we are, we can make our alone time. We can have our walk going to or from something we need to do, we can be alone as we work in the yard, as we drive. We can be alone when there are people around us. We may be like a young mother with four tiny children. She makes her alone time by sitting in the middle of the floor and putting her apron over her head. This is the signal that mother is not to be talked to until the apron comes down. Today we enjoy being alone, alone with God.

## We Can Know

Dear Friend,

When we need to find something, need to find out something and it seems impossible, what can we do? It may be there is very little time. We may need to know or to find something right away. Someone may be waiting for us to find it. We may need an answer immediately. We may be in a state of panic.

So we calm.

We quiet down our mental activity. We pacify our fears of not finding. We get still and we remember that God in us knows where what we need is. God knows the answer, God can give us directions to where we need to be. *God in us knows.* God in us wants us to have the answer. God waits for us to be still so that we can remember that God is there so God can tell us. Until we remember, until we are still, God can't. So whatever our need is now for direction, whatever that need is at this time, we stop all activity for the moment. We get physically still, we get emotionally still, we get mentally still, and, as we relax, we pray, "Father-Mother God, thank You for being with me all the time. Thank You for all Your knowingness. Thank You for Your wanting to direct me now. I am still and I give thanks for Your direction and guidance. My panic is gone. I know You know and tell me now." Often even non-praying people say, usually in desperation, "God knows." God does know and the wonder is God not only knows but God will let us know. Today we give thanks that this is so.

87

## No Dissapointments

Dear Friend,

Today we are thinking about changes in the weather and how we can adjust to them. We can adjust in different ways. We can put on warmer clothes or cooler ones. We can think it's getting winter time or it's getting summer and be happy about it and enjoy the change. We can shivver or perspire and make all kinds of complaining noises. Sometimes we react as if the change in the weather is a personal attack. Often our life weather changes too, and if we have learned to blend with the changes in weather we are more likely to be able to blend with other kinds of changes that come to us.

Disappointing news of an impending change comes. We do not consider it diasppointing, merely a change and we adjust. People we love move out of our life. We bless them, release and let them go and we adjust. A job changes. We do not bewail what has been. We look forward to the new. We adjust. We have to move, again we have a choice. Do we let ourselves be upset? Today we adjust to changes in the weather and changes in our lives. God helps us.

God is everywhere, God is in change. Our remembering this lets God help us find good in our change. We have to choose good in the change. Choice is using our free will. When we remember, good comes easily and quickly from all changes. And the good in the change can happen easier and faster.

## Changes Can Be Good

Dear Friend,

Often our days do not go the way we plan or the way we think we want them to go. Sometimes our weeks and months change from expectations. Sometimes we feel our lives are not going as we think they should and are not going as we want them to go. Sometimes as we look back on a day or a week or a year and think of changes that came and we remember plans that never came about, we realize that what happened we could not have planned, but it added good things to our lives. More often we are likely to be belligerent about changes. We wanted to do what we planned. We don't like having our plans get pushed out of shape. What can we do?

We need plans, we need to accomplish desires, goals. We start by asking God to design our days, asking God to plan what we are going to do and to experience, asking God to put the value on happenings in our lives and days. We pray, "Father-Mother God, I am letting You decide what is important for me to experience and do today. I am making the best plans I can but I am receptive to changes You bring. I will not let changes, additions to or subtractions from my planned day and life bother me. I will accept them as gifts from You. I will know that You are putting the truly important things in the right order of my days."

We give thanks that God will. We keep on planning and then let God help with the fulfillment—and oh the difference!

## Don't Demote God

Dear Friend,

Someone has said that when we express fear, we demote God. When we allow ourselves to be afraid we are saying God isn't great enough, God doesn't know enough, God isn't able to protect us, to guide us to safety or do whatever needs to be done to help us get away from whatever is feared by us. Demoting God? Isn't that something? Who are we to think we can demote God? Who are we to try to take from God? Who are we to think that God isn't the highest, the top power, the head wise one, the one who loves more than anyone else? We really should laugh at our temerity, laugh at our audacity to demote God!

If there is anything in our lives right now that is scary, anything at all that we are afraid of, whether it is of a circumstance or possible happening, whether it is a person, whether it is a job at the moment we don't feel we can handle, it doesn't matter. We are not going to be afraid another moment because we are accepting the laughable possibility that in this fear, in allowing this fear to be, we are demoting God, we are putting something, our fear, above God.

We are putting God in second place and you and I have a first class God who will protect and provide for us.

## God, You Handle Today

Dear Friend,

Let this be a day of letting God handle us and everything and everybody in our lives. We say and mean, "God, You handle me today. Handle me in everything I do and say. Handle my feelings and my thoughts too. I give you complete permission to handle me today. Thank You for handling me in Your wonderfully perfect way all day today."

As the day progresses, we say and pray, "God, You handle this. I may think that I know what to do about this but that doesn't matter. You handle it. Then I'll know if what I think is right. Thank You for handling this for me."

We are not going to turn over to God only sticky messes and burdens and obstacles, but we're going to hand over seemingly easy to handle things, hand it all over to God. God has this wonderful way of making even good better, the happy even happier, the beautiful more beautiful, so we say, "God, handle this. It looks O.K. It looks good but You can make it even better."

We remember to let God handle everything, our indispositions, our frets, our irritation, our fears, our joys, our excitements, our decisions, our bodies, our minds, our emotions. What a day we are going to have!

## More Than 50 Percent

Dear Friend,

A young woman in Puerto Rico told me that before she and her husband were married, the priest told each of them separately that each must want to give and give more than 50 percent. When there was need for forgiveness to go more than 50 percent of the way, take more than 50 percent of the blame, to think only of how to add more than 50 percent to the marriage. Marriage is no problem when each gives more than 50 percent. Life is no problem when we give more than 50 percent.

We stop thinking of keeping things even. We stop questioning what another has done for us. All we have to do is to be sure that we are giving more than 50 percent in every part of our life. More attention, more praise, more appreciation, more encouragement, more help, more love, more kindness, more consideration.

Right now we give complete attention to our Father-Mother God and say, "Thank You, Father-Mother God for helping me give as You do. You give 100 percent. I want Your help to give more than 50 percent. Thank You."

Today we emphasize giving and let receiving take care of itself. "Today I give more than 50 percent. I give more than 50 percent."

## Patience

Dear Friend,

Many of us have difficulty with patience. We want to be. We try to be but we aren't always patient. To be patient is a matter of focus. How are we looking at the situation tempting us to be impatient? Are we seeing what is important? Are we seeing only the close and immediate? Are we seeing results? We may grab something and ruin it. We may slap someone and start something big. We may be impatient and spoil dinner. Results may be a break up of a marriage, friendship, job, a car mishap.

Oh, what impatience does to us physically. We've had an emotional explosion and it is fatiguing. It drains us and then we have emotional after effects of shame, guilt, remorse. Impatience is not worth its cost. The bad effects of impatience last, last much longer than any delay.

Patience is beautiful, patience gets things done, patience doesn't break things or hurt people. Patience leaves everyone feeling good, especially us when we have been patient.

God is a God of patience; therefore, we have in us God patience. We can let this God attribute that is ours express. You and I can be patient, we can let the God of patience work in us and through us until we no longer feel impatient or express impatience. Today can be a day of wonderful, rewarding patience.

## Facing People

Dear Friend,

Frequently you and I want to avoid certain people. We don't want to avoid them because they are bad or ugly or smell bad. We avoid them because we don't want to face them. We may not want to be reminded of unpleasant times with them. We may not want to face that we have not been right with them. We're hiding. We're hiding not as much from them as from ourselves. If we avoid them we don't have to think right now about something that is unfinished business.

Business is always unfinished until we have faced ourselves and then faced whatever we need to face to get ourselves clear from the past. We're really not reluctant about seeing these people; we're reluctant about seeing ourselves as we are with them. The truth is we don't need to be afraid. We can have a household or office clutter or even disaster. Things may be piled and impossible but with physical matters we usually can start and the mess gets cleared up. We want to do the same with this.

If we haven't fulfilled an obligation, if we have been angry, if we have said things we shouldn't, if we have hurt someone, if we have not told the truth, we face it, we admit it, do what we can and then let it go, but not hide. Criminals find it hard to stay hidden. We find it painful. We find it disrupting our peace of mind and hurting our effectiveness. Today we stop avoiding, stop hiding. God will help us face ourselves and then face the situation.

## Not Control

Dear Friend,

Today let's think of the difference between mind control and using the power of the mind. A controlled anything is not as wonderful as something that is used. A horse that has to be controlled is not the same joy and delight as a horse that can be guided gently. When we try to control our minds we are not letting them be free to expand. We do not want to clamp them down. We do not want to be heavy handed with our minds. We want our minds to know that we appreciate them, that we are going to try to use their unlimited power to work for us to go in good directions.

When we control something there is always the danger of what it is we are controlling getting out of our control. We don't want that. We want the marvelous mind power to be of use to us in beautiful ways and it will as we think of using it and not controlling it. There is such a basic difference between being controlled and being guided. We want to guide our minds, we want to make use of them. Today we use our minds, use our minds more than we did yesterday or any other yesterday. Use them to bring about the good that we want. Use them to picture good coming to us, use them to anticipate good, use them to give us wonderful creative ideas.

We are not heavy handed with our minds, we are light handed, sure handed. We direct and guide, we do not control. Today we use our minds and wonderful things happen.

## Storms Subside

Dear Friend,

When we feel ourselves getting upset, too excited, angry, disturbed in any way, there is one easy way for us to get at peace. We turn from what it is that we are allowing to annoy us and think first about what this is doing to our bodies. We usually find that we are breathing rapidly, with quick, shallow breaths, and our heart has accelerated its pumping rate.

We turn attention to our heart. It is pumping our life blood through us, blood to our arms and legs, blood to our brain, everywhere in us. It is pumping life. Now we are going to think of its aiding that life by knowing that each beat brings us peace. We visualize the blood as a carrier of peace, as flowing peace and each beat of our heart keeps that peace flowing.

Our breathing will slow as we know that this vital breath of life is bringing not only the life sustaining air but it is bringing in air that holds peace. Instead of feeling the air coming into us we are starting to feel peace coming in. Each breath is a breath of peace, each heartbeat one of peace.

Now we can remember the great gift Jesus the Christ gave us. He told us he was giving us peace, His perfect, wonderful, never failing, always available peace. Feeling peace coming into our bodies with every breath, every heart beat, we can accept the gift of the Christ and we are at peace.

## Inflow/Outflow

Dear Friend,

Today we expect more from life, more out of life, and we expect to give more to life and for life. Always there must be this balance, the outflow and the inflow. Let's think about the things that we are going to expect to come in increasing amounts and kinds for us.

We want the more abundant life, the rich life. We want more happiness, greater health, more money, more success, more wisdom, more friends, more love, more fun. Perhaps some of these we want more or feel we need more than the others. Whatever we decide right now that we want more of, this is what we are going to desire today, this is what we are going to expect coming to us today . . . coming to us in beautiful, wonderful ways bringing only happiness and joy with them. This is the first part of our part in bringing greater good into our experience. Then we have to give out to life.

We want more strength and health, so we care for our bodies with right food, drink, exercise, rest, appreciation, love. If it is financial then we think rich, bless, give thanks and appreciate what we now have and give out in some way, give more than we have been, do better work on the job, more for others. We work to find employment where we can serve best. Today is our day to expect and to help bring about increased abundance of every good thing into our lives and affairs.

## Our Peace Angel

Dear Friend,

Let's think about the angel who passed over the troubled water and the water became still. It's a beautiful picture—stormy waters, white caps, high waves, water coming higher and higher on the shore. Then there is the angel. The waters respond to the peace of the angel and become still. We can superimpose this picture on our life today.

Whenever there seems to be toubled water, we can invite our angel of peace to come and still the disturbance. We may have troubled thoughts, fears perhaps, hurts, angers, sadness. And we have not been able to calm these thoughts and feelings but our angel of peace can. Right now we invite our own, our very own angel of peace and love, to calm these thoughts and feelings that are keeping us upset. Our angel bringing our peace will come.

Perhaps it is a situation in business or family and we've tried to take care of it. God's angel of peace and love will come at our bidding and calmness will come. All the noise of disturbance, all the hot words and tempers, all the friction will calm. We pray together, "Father-Mother God, thank You for Your angels of peace and love." Our special angel will come. Sometimes we think it may take two or more angels. If it does, they will come. We visualize them, we feel the soft flutter of angel wings of peace and love and all becomes as it should be.

## Double Minded

Dear Friend,

We're going to think about seeing both good and evil. Doublemindedness. Our doublemindedness not simply Adam and Eve's doublemindedness that got them out of the Garden of Eden. Our doublemindedness that keeps us out of our own Garden of Eden. Our doublemindedness that often we don't realize we have. Most of us have been brought up by people who are doubleminded. Now we are learning to be singleminded. We do not ignore the non good. It is a fact but it is changeable. Good is the real and the permanent, the eternal. Good is possible in every situation because God is there.

God is there because God is everywhere. The not good can change. Facts change all the time. Where we live can change. The new address and the old address are both true for the time we live at each. Addresses change. Our home we have with us always. The amount of money in our billfold and bank account can vary. Substance we always have access to. Health can vary, facts of health, but God's life is ours. Friends can be here and there but love never leaves us.

How are we looking at things? Are we seeing facts that can change or bad and good. We check today. We want to keep our eyes on good. This is single vision. We can.

## Deciding Thoughts

Dear Friend,

We are going to remember all day that our thoughts are ours to use. There is no limit to our thoughts. They don't cost us anything but they can be costly. If we think the wrong kind of thoughts, unhappy things can happen. Thoughts are free and we are free to use them in any way. However, we do not always use them so that they will bring about good in our lives.

We remember that it is only in our mind that we have full control. It is the only place where other people do not have power over us in any way unless we let them. This is our kingdom. This is where we reign. Our thoughts can be as we want them to be and we can choose our thoughts. Right thoughts bring good.

Today we remember and we watch our thoughts. We think of the power of each thought. It will keep us from thinking thoughts that are really thoughtless because they have been thought without any conception of their power or what they are going to bring in to our experience.

No matter if we have been allowing our thoughts to run wild, be negative, fearful, resentful, impatient, we can tell them what to do now. Today we take charge of our thinking and happy, rich wonderful things happen. We use our thoughts today to make our lives happy in every good way. God will help us direct our thoughts toward good.

## Run Your Own Race

Dear Friend,

The coach of the winner of five medals in the Winter Olympics told him not to let other racers determine how he would run but "to run his own race." We need to run our own race. We will when we realize that we do not need to compete, we only need to develop our potential, our God-given uniqueness. Then we will be gold medal winners. Too often we do let others determine what we are going to do, how and when. We don't need to do this.

As we keep close to our Father-Mother God, we will know what it is we are to do. We will find every day is planned in the best way. We will find opportunities come to us when we are ready. We find help when we need it. To run our own race does not mean that we are going to think we know exactly what to do and get determined, perhaps even belligerent about it. No, instead we give our lives to God so that the Divine Plan in us can unfold easily and perfectly.

We do not let others tell us what to do. We listen, we think about what they say. We get still and put it up for God's deciding. If others are going at life in a way they think is right for them, it can be. It may not be for us. We do not think anyone is further ahead than we are or that we have to be like them to succeed, to gain more wisdom and understanding, anything. God will help us run our own race successfully.

## It's All Right

Dear Friend,

It took me quite some time to get to the place where I could say and mean it, understand it when I said, no matter what was happening or being said, "It's all right." Everything really is all right because God is everywhere and because God is everywhere, good has to be there regardless of appearances. We say that God is omnipresent, everywhere equally present, so everywhere there is good. Everywhere there is good despite ugly, awful, horrible appearances. Remembering and recognizing that despite appearances God is still there helps God make things the way they should be.

We were given free will, choice, and when we choose to remember that God is in all people and all things, we help free God activity that cannot be free unless we free it. Oh, how free we become when we know this, know it not only intellectually but know it with all of our being. "It's all right. God is here, God is there. God is in this. Good will come through this because God is here." We say it, we give thanks for God activity's taking over and we expect good, good that we cannot see yet, and good comes.

I have seen so much good come through frightening experiences, through sudden threatening situations. Good has a hard time coming unless we call it and we call it forth, we welcome it, we affirm our faith in it, when we remember to say, "It's all right."

## Power in Praise

Dear Friend,

There is power in praise. Praise is strong, not flattery. Often we withhold deserved praise because we fear it will seem flattery. Praise calls forth the best in people. Praise encourages. Everything and everyone responds to praise. When we do not praise we are withholding good from others, good which they should have and need. We can increase the good of what we praise, increase the good of the person or we can decrease it by not giving it. Not only are we keeping deserved praise from being given we are cutting down our own good.

What we give returns to us. If we give praise and recognize good in others and good in what they are doing, we will have a return. Praise helps us recognize good. When we praise our bodies for what they do for us, our bodies respond by doing better jobs of maintaining and improving our health. Praise calls forth good as well as recognizing good. Praise is power. We remember Paul and Silas in prison sang and praised God. The power was so strong that there was an earthquake and their chains fell off. They were free. Praise frees us in many ways.

Praise frees us from jealousy, praise frees us from self-centeredness. Praise frees us from seeing the negative. Praise changes people. Giving praise changes us. It opens us up to seeing good and expecting good. As we praise, we feel its power and we begin to experience only good because we see only good.

## Bouncing Back

Dear Friend,

Soon after the oleander bushes outside my window started to bloom in a profusion of rose red, heavy rain came. The blossoms ducked their head and let the rain come down. The heads stayed down the two days the rains continued. Dry days again and up came the heads. They bounced back in all their beauty. By ducking they did not lose many rosy petals. Today there was more heavy rain. The heads went down. The sun is out and the heads are up. They've bounced again.

They did not defy the rain, they didn't stand up against it. We can do the same thing when difficulties appear. We can let them "rain" on us and then we can bounce back. To fight circumstances, to get angry, to get even does no good. They only wear us out and we are as bedraggled as these oleander blossoms would be if they had tried to take on the rain.

We can seem not to be doing anything about situations that threaten. But we bide our time. We do nothing at the moment. Then we will know what we are to do. We will not be worn out, we will not have done and said things we regret, we will be ready and in good shape to handle whatever the situation. We remember the oleander blooms. They duck during the storms and then they rise up, strong, unhurt, ready to do their job giving the world their beauty. Each of us has particular beauty and goodness to give the world and we'll do it successfully as we ride the storms with ease and then bounce back.

### 'Praise the Lord'

Dear Friend,

Have we praised God today? Have we thought of praising God? We need to get the feeling of praising, the habit of singing and praising God for many good reasons. God is the Source of all our good. God's wisdom is ours to use. God life is for us to use. God's love is for us to enjoy. God has every good thing for us. How good it feels when we think to praise God, when we think to sing God's praises. Everything improves and increases with praise.

Our good will multiply as we see its Source is God. We will have such a good feeling inside when we praise our Father-Mother. When we praise we get a warm feeling, we fill filled with joy and love and thanksgiving. People used to say, "Praise the Lord." Sometimes that was said without feeling and the phrase became a cliché. We do not need to go around shouting, "Praise the Lord." The shouting and the singing should be in our minds and hearts. Praising God is a habit. It is a habit that we can start right now.

We think of all the good in our lives, we think of the good that has come about today—already. And then we think, "I am going to praise God for this." As we do this we begin to know that wonders will never cease. Praising God accelerates God activity in our lives and good mushrooms.

## Persist, Persevere

Dear Friend,

Two wonderful words are "persist" and "persevere." We need them both if we are to accomplish aims and dreams. It is easy for us to stop and not complete tasks. It is easy for us to think things are taking too long. It is easy for us to allow discouragement. Sometimes we pray and if nothing happens at once, we say "prayer doesn't work." If we want a healing and it doesn't come quickly, we think it's not coming. There are reasons why things do not come about rapidly.

Usually our aims and dreams involve other people and all have to be in right relationship at the right place before things can happen. There is a time for things to happen. Often there are things for us to learn, things for us to experience before we are ready. We keep on. We persist in our prayers, we persist in our expectation of good. We do not allow discouragement. We persist. We persevere. We keep on regardless of the time it takes, regardless of seeming setbacks.

We don't want to give up on good. We don't want to let our dreams disappear. We persist. We hold our dream in front of us. We hold it high. We keep on knowing each delay is a time for our learning more to help the dream. We persist in our prayers, we persist in our working toward our goals. We do not allow discouragement, we do not throw our dreams away. We persist. We persevere.

## Wrong Decision?

Dear Friend,

What do we do if we have made what appears to be a wrong decision? Instead of wasting time in regret and chastizing ourselves for being so stupid, we do the practical thing: we make another decision. We can always make another decision. One decision does not end all. Often we make what seems to turn out to be a wrong decision. We prayed about it, thought prayerfully about it, and still it was evidently the wrong thing. We remind ourselves that God hasn't changed.

God is still with us. God will still help us with our decisions and God does not condemn us for not having heard the right decision. God isn't going to take away His help. And it may not be a completely wrong decision. Things may happen because of it that are very good and that could not have happened if we had not made that particular decision. One thing for sure we are going to learn from this, and this is very valuable. It can be the foundation for our not making other and larger wrong decisions. We can say, "No, I've been down that road." So today we bless every wrong decision we think we have made.

We decree we are going to make good decisions from now on because we are going to listen to God. We will try to hear God's decision but we know we can make another if we don't!

## How Do I Feel?

Dear Friend,

Today I exercise my freedom to choose how I feel about everything. I start right now where I am. How do I feel about the next thing I have to do whether it is to get up and get the day started or go to sleep or any thing? What is the next thing to do? How am I looking at it? Am I giving it a good name, a good expectation or am I calling it bad names? Do I have a feeling of dread or resentment about the next task? Or do I think it's going to be good to get it done? Am I thinking, "I don't know if I can do what I've got to do," or "I don't have to do this alone for God is with me to give me ideas and to give me strength, and it will get done." Am I trying to avoid doing something that I should do, or am I saying, "I am going to get this done right now." Do I want to avoid meeting or talking with someone? Or do I think, "Something good is going to come out of this meeting, and I'm going to enjoy it."

That word "enjoy" is important. Are we feeling enjoyment as we look ahead to our activities today? We can because enjoyment starts in expectation, how we feel about what is ahead. With God's help not only can we do what we need to do today, but we can find joy in it because God is joy and there is joy in doing. There is great joy in doing what we may not, at first, feel like doing. Today we feel there will be joy for us in everything we do.

## Cause and Effect

Dear Friend,

Today let's think how wonderful it is that there is a dependable law of cause and effect. We want to give thanks today and every day that always there is a cause and always there is an effect. It helps us understand things that happen to us and in the world. It helps us change ourselves and our world because if effect always follows cause then we can change causes and effects will be different.

If we realize that our feeling listless all day is because we stay up to see late movies, then we either take a nap earlier or turn the television off earlier. If we feel others are avoiding us, we listen to ourselves. Are we irritable, complaining, always seeing the negative? We want to be wanted and liked so we stop complaining, we stop seeing something wrong with everything and everybody.

If we are not experiencing prosperity we start doing, thinking, feeling things that attract prosperity.

Today we look at our lives as effects of our causes. Then we decide on needed changes so effects can be different. God will help us. God wants us have only good effects and God has given us tools to bring good effects in our lives and today we use them.

## See the Wonder

Dear Friend,

Today let's look at others seeing what they will become and let us be amazed at the wonder of their becoming. It is not easy for us to see people and situations, even ourselves in any way except as we are at this moment. We treat tomatoes better than we treat ourselves or other people.

A friend said, "I have six tomato plants. I'll not be buying tomatoes this summer and you'll have tomatoes too." She wasn't seeing that little plant that was perhaps six inches tall and a bit spindly. She was seeing a tall, full grown plant loaded with beautiful red tomatoes. It doesn't bother us that a baby is a baby, a six year old a six year old. It shouldn't bother us that we are not perfect yet, that we still have lessons to learn, that we still have accomplishments to achieve and it should not bother us that others aren't perfect yet.

Today we start our thinking ahead not stopping at now. And we pray, "Father-Mother God, I need new vision so that I can see myself as I am going to be as I learn more, as I become better every way. I need new vision so I can see those around are learning and growing too and I want a glimpse of the perfection they are going to be. Thank You for helping me make this a day of seeing my becoming and the becoming of others." This will help us all become what we are to be.

## Safety In Faith

Dear Friend,

Let's think for a bit about the safety there is in faith. Faith is the surest safety we can have. Faith makes us safe from so many things. Faith makes us safe from worry. When we have faith in God and faith in ourselves, faith in good, faith in good coming through every happening, every condition, we no longer have anything to worry about. So faith saves us from sleepless nights, saves us from getting worry wrinkles and tense bodies. Faith makes us safe from fear of any kind. If we are in a dangerous situation, even if we are alone to face that physical danger, if we stay with our faith we can know that we will come through safely.

Faith makes us safe from doubt about our ability. When we rely on our faith and have faith to rely on we will know that God in us will help us do all that we are to do and that God already has given us a plan to succeed. We will be safe from negative responses and reactions when we have faith. With faith one cannot be irritable, impatient, angry. With faith one cannot be unloving.

Today we feel the safety of faith. We think about it. We give thanks that we have our God to have faith in. We give thanks that we were so created that we can have faith in our body's healing power, faith in our creative power to create a life we want, conditions we want. Today we are safe, we have faith and we give thanks for it.

111

## No Loss

Dear Friend,

Today we are going to think about "No loss." It can be difficult to believe there is no loss when there is every appearance of loss. Friends or relatives may be gone. Death may happen, divorce, misunderstandings, a job. Possessions or money may be gone. How can we entertain the possibility that there is no loss? We forget at such times that we are heirs to all that God has and that God knows all things and God has all power. This means that God has replacement, God can find the lost, God can make all right.

There is only one Substance. Scientists call it one energy and tell us there is no destruction of this energy only change in form. We think then of this loss as change in form. Lost articles will be found or replacements will come easily and wonderfully. A new job will be found. If a mate, friend, relative is gone and we face change, then we take care of it by knowing there is still happiness and love for us. After a loss in money, we know there will be more and we have learned through this experience. We will be richer for it. Change brings newness. God's plenty is for us always. Today we pray and sing, "Thank God there is no loss. There is only change. There is no loss." And new good comes.

## Comfort

Dear Friend,

Sometimes we need comforting more than anything else. Sometimes we need reassurance. Sometimes we need to feel someone close, someone who will not judge us, criticize us, or make demands upon us. Sometimes we feel battered and bruised and we need, we long for comfort. And we can have it.

We can have the comfort we need and desire. It is always ready for us. We turn to the Father-Mother God within us and all around us. We turn to a love that is everlasting, unchanging, all caring, and desiring all good for us. We accept that love. We begin to feel it as perhaps we haven't before or have forgotten how comforting God's love feels.

We remember the many times as a child we had the comforting love of our parents. We remember when husband, wife or friend comforted us. We remember how we relaxed into that love and we do now as we pray, "Father-Mother God, I am crying out for comfort. My body needs it, my emotions need it, my mind needs it. I know you love me and have comfort for me. I open myself up to receive it. Thank You."

We will be comforted.

113

## A Joyful Noise

Dear Friend,

We are told frequently in Psalms to make a joyful noise unto the Lord. The Psalmist talks of his joy as he sings unto the Lord. Part of the joy of living is feeling alive and vital. To sing joyously makes us feel alive and vital. It is difficult for us to have a feeling of joy when our bodies are sluggish or hurting, but we can help our bodies be vital and live and healthy by being joyous. Joy frees the body to function as it was created. By being joyful, even if we don't feel alive and vital, helps our bodies start feeling that way.

Our being joyful helps the healing life energy in us start to heal, renew, restore, re-energize, purify. It's a wonderful complete circle: we are joyful when we feel alive and vital, and we get alive and vital when we feel joyous! No matter which comes first, results are the same— we are alive and vital. So we make a joyful song today.

We don't need to burst into an aria or even a lullaby but we will speak and sing joyfully. Our voices will vibrate with joy. We will say joyously, "I am happy. I love you. I feel great. Today is a wonderful day. I feel wonderful. I am happy." Today is beautiful, wonderful. Everything good is happening, and it will be as we feel joyous, alive and vital and make joyful noises unto the Lord.

"Today I sing."

## Only The Wind

Dear Friend,

Sometimes we are awakened in the night by a disturbing sound. Then we realize that it is only the wind banging a branch agasin the roof. We are relieved, we go back to sleep feeling safe and comfortable. When things threaten us and we respond in instant fear, we remember the wind. We say to ourselves, "This is only the wind."

Events, rumors, circumstances can seem threatening, menacing, but we dissipate our fears by knowing these are only sounds of the wind of fear. In Truth it is only the wind. The wind will die down and, even if it still blows, we know our safety, we know where our refuge is. We are safe. Anyone we may have been fearful about is safe.

What is happening, what is being said, what is being felt is only the noise of the wind, only the banging of the wind against other consciousnesses. The wind we are hearing in our world will die down, calm will come, the noise and the banging will be over, the fear, the threat, the menace all will be gone.

The wind blows and the wind stops. The noise is and the noise isn't. We are all right. We are with God. God is with us. We can say about anything that is disturbing, "It's only the wind." Thank God.

# Re-Focusing

Dear Friend,

When we are concerned about something that is happening in our lives, when we find that we are scared or worried, angry or resentful, we need to refocus. We need to start looking for something good in our lives. We need to focus on the many blessings there always are in our lives. Something happens when we change our attention focus. Something very good happens when we pay attention to good. Our attention activates good, invites it, and good starts happening.

As we do this, we find that there is almost an instant reversal of our feelings. The situation may not have changed, but we will. When we focus on something else and then look again at our problem, we will not be putting one picture on top of another, we will not be putting a good picture on a bad one or a positive on top of a negative. We will be removing our emotional involvement. We will break the spell emotions put on us. We will be free to think clearly and to hear Inner Direction. We will be able to know what to do about things with God's help.

Then it will be easy for us to remember that God is always with us to help in whatever situation we find ourselves. God's wisdom is always for us to use and we can after we have refocused.

Today we refocus. It helps if we say often, "I do not keep my attention on my worries or angers. I refocus on the good and good happens."

### Publius Was Right

Dear Friend,

Along time ago Publius Syrus said a number of wise things that have lasted through the centuries. One is, "In quarreling, truth is always lost." We tend to think that in anger out comes truth. That truth is the kind of resentment we have been harboring and it may or may not be based on facts. We know, you and I, that when we are angry logic goes out. We know that we exaggerate, we color what has happened with our emotions. In anger we lose perspective, we lose all sense of proportion. We lose truth. Most of us are honest and want to be. It can help us not be angry if we remember that if we allow anger we are in danger of losing our self-respect because we cannot have self-respect if we are dishonest.

Deciding if what we are expressing is honest will give us time to cool emotion. It will give us time to "count to 10." It will give us opportunity to find logic. It will, without doubt, give us wisdom to take care of the situation without anger.

Our bodies will bless us. They will not have to take the brunt of what anger does. Our hearts will, our blood pressure will. It will give us time for a quick prayer, "Father-Mother God, am I being honest? Am I losing truth? I want to be honest. I want to be right, Show me how." God will. We remember Publius Syrus and give thanks for him today.

# Old Out, New In

Dear Friend,

It is easy to see the truth of life in one context and not in another. We can know that we have got to get old grass off the yard before new grass can grow, and we have to keep weeds out of the garden before vegetables have a chance. We know old oil has to be drained out of a car before new can be put in. We can forget that the same law of getting rid of the old before there can be new good holds in every part of our life.

We have to get rid of old ideas of lack before we can have thoughts of prosperity. We have to get rid of old sadness before we can take in new happiness. We have to get rid of old hates and resentments before we can have room for new peace of mind and heart. We have to throw out thoughts of injustice before thoughts of justice can find room. We have to get rid of fears before we can act with courage.

Today we check ourselves out as we would a closet, a business, a car. What is cluttering us up? What is crowding out good in our lives? What needs to be thrown out? We're the closet, the car, the business. We toss out the old, unwanted and unneeded. We make room for the new and beautiful, the new and happy, the new and healthy, the new and prosperous. We give thanks that we can clean out the old and have the new. Today we do.

## We Prophesy

Dear Friend,

All of us have a natural curiosity about the future. When we read a story we are eager to find out how it is going to turn out. We'd like to know our future. This is natural. What happens in our lives is important to us. This is why many of us would like to have a personal prophet, someone who could tell us what will happen if we do certain things or if we don't. The truth of it is that we do have a prophet, our very own prophet.

There is in us that which can forecast success or failure, happiness or unhappiness, sickness or health. We can predict good for ourselves or we can predict the not good. We can predict success and abundance and joy or we can predict failure, lack and depression. We do this by the way we think and speak and feel.

What we say we expect, what we say about ourselves, how we feel about ourselves, determines our todays and tomorrows. Jesus the Christ said that by our words are we justified, and by our words we are condemned.

So today we are careful that we do not let unhappy words about ourselves or our prospects cross our lips but only words, thoughts and feelings of confidence, trust, happy expectancy, reliance on the Father-Mother within. We realize we prophesy our future. We are our own prophets.

## Mistakes Can Go

Dear Friend,

It is good to remember that when we stop making any mistake, results from the mistake stop too. Think back to simple arithmetic. Once we knew our multiplication table, we no longer made any mistakes in multiplying and dividing. It is the same in all areas and aspects of our life.

Once we know what we have been doing that is interfering with our health, happiness, or prosperity, we can stop that interference. Not only does our stopping mistakes in thinking and feeling, speaking and acting help us now, it does more. It starts erasing results of past mistakes.

Today we can know as we eliminate mistakes in our way of approaching life, we also eliminate effects of previous mistakes. We free ourselves today from previous and present misuse. This is what we want and we pray for help: "Father-Mother God, thank You for helping me understand my mistakes and help me eliminate them. I know that, as I do, the effects I have been experiencing will stop. Only I can eliminate my own mistaken attitudes, eliminate my negative emotions, thoughts, words and actions. And I can with Your help. Thank You."

God will help us every minute when we seek and reach out for God help in eliminating mistakes and avoiding new ones. It will be easier than we think.

We affirm: "I am free from mistakes and results of mistakes."

120

## Remember: Pick Up Your Good

Dear Friend,

We write our name on our good, no one else does. Our health doesn't come because someone else cares that we do health bringing things, eat right, exercise right, sleep enough. Our financial success doesn't come because someone wants to see us successful. Our happiness doesn't come because someone else says, "Be happy." Our health, our personal success, our happiness, our every good comes only when we claim it, when we know that special good is for us.

We can claim good and never do anything about picking it up as we may order something through a Sears catalogue and never pick it up. I've known people who were eager to see how their pictures turned out and then never went by to pick up the finished film. Nearly every business man can tell us that people order merchandise and don't pick it up. Dry cleaners clean garments never collected. We can order our good and not pick it up. We can affirm it, we can picture it and then forget it.

We can pray for our good and, when it doesn't come quickly, we get discouraged or we worry about the matter, or we think it's too good to be true.

Your good and my good has our name on it but we have to claim it, we have to go to the trouble of staying with the claiming, have to do certain things to get it. Our good is waiting with our name on it. Today we do what we have to do, what we know to do to claim it. It's ours, ours to pick up.

## Talk to Self

Dear Friend,

We were brought up to think we should not talk to ourselves. Most of us were also told that, if we have to talk to ourselves, then we must be very careful not to answer ourselves. This is not true. This is not good advice because we need to learn to talk to ourselves. We must also listen to ourselves. There is this wonderful Self of us that is spirit, that is always in direct communication with our God and knows all things for us. We spell this Self with a capital S, for it is the Lord of our being, it is the God Self of us.

It is our dearest friend, it is our wisest friend, it is our most loving friend, our most caring friend, our most protective friend. Friends are to be talked to, friends are to be listened to and this Friend is always there to talk with us, to guide and direct us.

It is to this Friend we want to direct our wondering, our doubting, our questioning. We ask and then give our Friend opportunity to answer. We do not say our question and then start doing something else. We wait and we listen. We will hear Our Friend; our Self with a capital S, will answer.

Today we remember to ask our Self, our Friend, what we need to know and we let our Friend answer.

### Follow or Walk With?

Dear Friend,

Today let's think about Jesus the Christ's telling his disciples to follow Him. We are likely to think that we are to try to live as Jesus did in our little way, doing the best we can but following a long way behind. We may feel it is a little like trying to follow a lead car in traffic. Sometimes we can keep the car ahead in view and sometimes cars get in between and we lose sight.

Instead of thinking we are behind Jesus today, let's think instead of how we use the words "follow me" with someone. Someone needs to find something in a store and we know our way around or in the office or school or plant where we work. We try to tell them how to go and we say, "Oh, come with me. Follow me." We mean "come with me" rather than "follow me." We mean "walk with me," "stay close to me" rather than stay behind and try to keep me in vision. We want them close. It's easier to direct people who are near.

Jesus the Christ must have meant this. Today we think Jesus wants us close to Him so that we can more easily know His directions and guidance, feel His love and caring, His protection, His joy. Today we do not follow behind Jesus the Christ, we quickly walk up, get close to Him in our prayers and meditation so that we are very near, nearer than we have ever been before. Today we come close to and we walk with the Christ. We feel the closeness.

## Lightfooted Ideas

Dear Friend,

Let's think about ideas today. Ideas are funny things. They won't work if we don't. They come when we least expect them and then they are gone, unless we give them an invitation to stay by doing something about them.

Ideas are lightfooted. They come in without our having any notice they are coming, and, if we don't make haste to do something about them they are gone. At the moment we believe we will not forget them and they will be there when we get around to using them. But they don't wait. They leave without a trace.

Ideas come to us from God. They come to help us do good things for us and for others. They come to have us do things at the right time, and the right time is always now, either the right time for action or preparation for action.

Ideas are to consider. Ideas are to explore. Ideas are to use. Toynbee has said that an idea that does not go into action is a failure. Any idea that is not acted upon is lost. Today with God's help we capture ideas. We consider them. We do something about them. And we pray, "Father-Mother God, thank You for all the ideas You send me today. I will appreciate them. I will appreciate them by doing something about them. Thank You."

## Enthusiasm

Dear Friend,

Samuel Ullman has written that to give up enthusiasm wrinkles the soul. Isn't that graphic? We know life loses vitality, beauty and wonder when we let our enthusiasm go. Without enthusiasm we cannot get much done; we don't reach out for the new; we recede. It is likely that losing enthusiasm does wrinkle our souls. We would not want to have a wrinkled soul. Not you, not me.

We want our souls smooth, happy, healthy, expanding, not drying up, wrinkled. If we are not feeling very enthusiastic today, we can be. Enthusiasm doesn't come to us. It has to be welcomed, invited to enter our minds and hearts. Yes, enthusiasm is always with us waiting and wanting to help us be exuberant about life and living.

We make this our prayer, "Father-Mother God, help me be enthusiastic about everything I do today. Help me greet people enthusiastically. Help me enjoy everything that happens today with enthusiasm. I do not want a wrinkled soul. I do not want to crimp the edges of my life. I want to enjoy life. I want enthusaism. With Your help, dear, Father-Mother, I can be enthusiastic and I can have enthusiasm."

## No More Hurt

Dear Friend,

Today let's think about what we can do when something hurts us and we thought we had reached the place where this kind of thing couldn't hurt us any more. We thought we had risen above being hurt. but it happened again. First we give thanks that we recognize the hurt and do not simply hurt. We remember we can be free from hurting.

We get busy and finish off the hurt. It's a little like cleaning an area and then seeing something we missed. It's not the big job it was and it doesn't mean that we have to go all over the area we cleaned. So with this. This hurt we didn't expect to come again doesn't mean that we have failed in our learning not to give others power to hurt us. It simply means we've got a little more denying any thing or anyone power to hurt us. It means more praying, more encouraging ourselves, more positive realization that no one and nothing can hurt us if we do not let them. We know we can take care of this little leak in our power. We can stop it.

We can reassert our control over our reactions. We reassert that we are going to be happy and not hurt no matter what anyone says or does. We'll find the new hurt goes. It can not return ever in full force for we will not allow it.

## Add 'Be Glad'

Dear Friend,

The other day I read a wonderful new way of saying, "Let go and let God." Too many of us say it so often that it can become a cliche. This new way will stimulate us and help us more completely let go and let God because this is telling us to let go, let God and be glad. Isn't that the way it should be?

Too often we say "Well, this is a last resort and I'm not sure but I will say it and I will try to think that God can take care of this." We are not really letting go but we will when we get glad.

Joy should come whenever we let go and let God. How wonderful to have a God we can give all our problems, all our hurts, all our confusions, all our decisions. Today we say many, many times, "Today, right now, I let all of the quandaries in my life go. I place them in God's hands and I rejoice and give thanks. I am glad. I am glad. I am glad." What a joyous song we will sing all day as we release all that needs releasing to God and let God take over. Our worries stop, our doubts stop.

Today we insure our gladness, we insure our faith, we insure the perfect outcome of everything in our lives because we are letting go and letting God take charge. We prove it by releasing and being glad.

## Walking Advertisements

Dear Friend,

In the television series La Fonz said in one program that when we put out an advertisement someone's going to buy. This is a graphic description of what happens to us. We continuously put out an advertisement and people will buy what we are selling about ourselves. If we are happy, self-assured, healthy, people are going to buy that we are a happy person who is self-assured and healthy and they will also buy that we are a valuable person and will want to hire us, make friends with us, be around us in a business or social way. If we are sarcastic, complaining, talking about our aches and pains, advertising other negative traits, then people will consider us that way.

They will buy what we are selling and they will not want to buy us. We are walking advertisements. We have a wonderful advertising director and we pray to our director right now, "Father-Mother God, I want to a walking, talking, living advertisement for you. I want to advertise only good. I do not want to advertise shoddy merchandise or negation of any kind. Thank You for helping me advertise only the good. Help me remember that I am advertising myself all the time." We want to look the good that we want to be and we thank La Fonz for bringing this truth to our attention.

## No Help in Worry

Dear Friend,

"Some of your hurts you have feared
And the sharpest you still have survived
But what torments of grief you endured
From evils which never arrived."
Emerson

How true. Our worst worries, our worst fears do not happen. We can learn to say, "This has not happened yet and it may not happen. Therefore I am going to stop worrying so I will be able to think clearly and be physically able to take care of it if it does." Then put it in God's hands, confident that there is no scary thing God cannot take the scare out of, there is no situation in which God cannot bring about the right solution. We have to do our part.

Our part is not to allow ourselves to worry or be scared and waste valuable time over something that may never come about. We have given it to God so it can never be the scary thing we have been imagining. Today we go about our work confident and happy.

We do what we can to be ready for whatever happens by trusting God, freeing our minds and bodies from worry, getting rest, living today to its happy fullest. Today we choose not to worry, we choose to keep ourselves happy and ready for all that comes. With God's help it will be good.

## Only Thorns

Dear Friend,

There are many, many ways we can react to things going on in our lives. Let us say that something good happens. We either accept it with or without gratefulness. We accept it as a lasting good or an unlasting one. We see only good in it or we see possibilities of not good in it. We let the good make us happy or not. And, if it is something that is an irritation or a disappointment or a hurt, how are we going to react? Do we allow ourselves to be devastated, get up in arms about it, get all tense or do we, as a friend said, consider it a thorn we've got to get out with the least pain.

We've all stepped on stickers, we've all been stuck by thorns. We can relate to her picture. We know that there are ways to get thorns out and there are ways that rip our skin. We don't want to rip ourselves any more than we can help over anything that happens. We know we need to take time, to go easy taking out stickers or thorns, we need a calm hand and we don't hurry. So with our life reactions. We don't get all excited, we don't do and say something fast. We get calm, we know there is time, time for us to pray before reacting, and we pray: "Father-Mother God, I want to be rid of this thorn. With Your help I can and I thank You." Ideas will come showing us how to handle the situation, how to react, how to get out the thorn that is hurting. It will be easier knowing they are only thorns, thorns we can remove without damage to us or anyone.

## We're Thieves?

Dear Friend,

You don't believe in stealing and neither do I. We know it is wrong to take things that don't belong to us. We also know that there are unpleasant results when we steal. There is always some kind of punishment. You and I don't consider oursrselves thieves, but most of us are. All of us, it is safe to say, are a special kind of thief. We can steal responsibility, responsibility that does not belong to us. We steal it every time we try to manipulate people for if they are manipulated by us then what they do is our responsibility. Every time we insist on our way, every time we try to force people to do something we want them to do or to do something in the way we want them to do it, we have stolen more responsibility. Every time we make up someone's mind, we have taken upon ourselves the responsibility for that decision. It becomes our decision, not theirs.

It's so easy for a parent to steal responsibility from a child, it's so easy for a husband or wife to steal from the mate, it's very easy to steal responsibility from a friend. We don't need it. If you and I were always right and if you and I were always asked what we think is best in any situation, then we might be safe to decide for others, but we are not always right, we are not often asked. So we stop deciding for others. We can put our family and our friends in God's care. We do not want any more responsibility. We don't want to be thieves.

## Move With the Light

Dear Friend,

Today we think about our shadows. They move with us as we move with the light. We want to be like our shadows and move with the light, with the light of God and we can. The God light is always ready to shine for us. We merely have to turn toward the light and let it shine. Then, as the light focuses on us and our world, on our day, we will know exactly where we are to go, which is the best direction for us to go.

We think about this Light that has a broader beam than any light we have ever turned on. In its beam we can see not only the way but we can see what is around that way, on either side and what lies ahead. The light gives us new and wonderful understanding of ourselves, what we are doing and where we are going and what lies ahead. This light will not only give us understanding of ourselves, but also of others and circumstances. It is an all revealing light.

It is a soft light, bright and soft, not harsh. Nothing hides from us when we let the light shine. It lights up the answers to questions and concerns.

We can enter a dark room and have to feel for the switch; the light comes instantly. We can reach for the switch to God light and instantly there will be wonderful light that will show us the way we are to go, will show us clearly our next steps. Today we move with the Light.

## Not Unfair

Dear Friend,

Today let's think about fairness, justice. Often we feel others aren't fair to us. Sometimes we feel life is unjust. Sometimes we call out "Why me?" "Why do I have to do everything." "Why not others?" "What have I done to deserve such treatment?" We can feel put upon and we can feel deprived and others aren't. In a marriage we can feel our mate has things so much easier. In a family we think that some get more than we do. It may seem that our friends find better bargains. Oh, how we can feel that we are getting the short end. We don't need to.

When we are tempted to react in a hurt or complaining way, to be indignant, we need to remember right then that we are God's beloved, that God is always fair, that God knows only justice. Then we know that God is always in every situation and if we think God is here then God is free to make good come from that short end we think we have been given. That short end may well be the rich end if we keep emotion out of our eyes so that we can see it. Often an unfair situation is really a protection. Often it leads to greater good, richer, more wonderful. Whatever in our lives now that does not seem fair, we bless and pray, "Father-Mother God, thank You for the good that is in this situation. I no longer think of it as unfair, unjust or as taking from me. I accept it as good. I accept and give thanks to You right now for the great, wonderful good that will come from it. You are fair and just and You are in charge. I trust You." We will feel better and good will come.

## Not Adopted

Dear Friend,

The other day I heard a preacher say that we were God's adopted children. My first reaction was "No, no we are God's for real children, God's natural children." I thought about the word adopted and wondered why this man had chosen it. Perhaps, I concluded, he meant that God has chosen us even as an adopted child is chosen. I could accept that but I still feel closer to my Father-Mother God by not putting that word "adopted" into our relationship. I do not feel adopted at all.

I feel a close definite parent-child relationship, one that has always been and always will be. With adoption there has not always been this relationship, we are indicating that there was a time when we weren't. And that is not so. We have always been God's children from the beginning and always will be. If there is anything in us that feels that we have not always been God's children, let's forget it now and open ourselves up to the beautiful Truth that we are, we always have been and we always will be God's children. This is who and what we are and it is wonderful.

Right now we say, "Thank You, Father-Mother God, that I am Your child. That I have always been and always will be. Thank You for loving me with Your everlasting love. No matter any separation I may have allowed myself to think and feel, it is not so. I have never been separated from You. I can never be. I am Your child always and always."

## Good 'I Won'ts'

Dear Friend,

Today you and I watch what we say "I won't" to. Most of us have a little of this "I won't" in us. It started in childhood. Some things we say "I won't" to we have to do. But we need to watch what we are protesting. Most aren't worth the protest but there are things we need to take a stand against. We can be very positive with our "I won'ts." Today we are. We can say and we need to say:

I won't be unkind for I am really a loving person.
I won't feel hurt for I know no one can hurt me unless I let them.
I won't be sick for God is my health.
I won't be unhappy for unhappiness shuts off my good.
I won't be ungrateful for I am truly an appreciative person.
I won't be unfair for I want always to be just.
I won't gossip or listen to gossip because I don't want to hurt anyone.
I won't be dishonest in any way for I am completely honest.
I won't claim anything I do not want. I will not say I am sick, tired or angry.

I will claim my good through using God's name, I Am, in only positive ways. Today I Am well, strong, rich, happy, free, wise, considerate, kind, loving, prosperous, successful, at peace with myself and everyone in my world.

## Wrong End

Dear Friend,

A friend told me that a woman who helped in their home used to say when someone was talking unhappy talk that they were talking from the wrong end of their mind. It makes a graphic picture, one that we can use to help us keep talking from the right end of our minds. We want to talk from happy, positive end of our minds, not the fault-finding, critical, complaining, unhappy end. Today let's think about our minds as being a line, one that we can choose our talking from, a line we can choose what kind of words we want to use, what kind of thoughts we want to express.

There's a lineup for us to choose from. Thoughts range from highly positive, happily expectant, faith-filled to doubting, fearful, negative, sad, depressed. They range from pleasant, peacefilled, harmonious to angry, belligerent, demanding, accusing, ugly. It can be very good for us to look at our thoughts as having this range of possibility and we keep reminding ourselves that we have a choice because we always have a choice.

That is one of our God-given gifts, freedom to choose how we are going to speak and feel. We choose the thoughts we want to think and, as we practice talking from the right end of our minds, we will find that all of our mind is becoming the right end. We thank our Father-Mother God, that we have been given choice. We are glad there is this right end of our mind to use to bring about good in our lives.

## Our Read Out

Dear Friend,

In computer language, our life is our read out. Our lives outpicture what is going on inside us. Our faces can be our read out for they show our happy thoughts, intense thoughts, worry thoughts, impatient thoughts or pouting thoughts. Our bodies show how much we are feeding them, exercising them, and resting them. They also tell if we are discouraged or angry. Circumstances in our lives can give us read out too.

It is good to study our read out, see what we are programming. We remember that we can cancel old programs, we can put in new programs. When we do, the read out changes. Our faces look different, our bodies, our lives, our finances too!

We remember we are children of God and heirs to our Father-Mother's riches of every kind. These riches come to us as ideas we can use to bring the good we need and desire. We always have our part to do. We get with it. We give thanks for new rich ideas, we follow Inner Direction and our read out changes. We continuously take a look at all of our life. We study the read out it gives us and we decide if we need to change our program or not. God will help us, God will bless us in any changes and in going on to ever greater good in every part of our life.

## No Fooling Around

Dear Friend,

Today we are going to think about "no fooling." We sometimes say this to a person we are talking with and we don't quite believe what we hear, and we tell children, "no fooling now." Today we tell ourselves, "no fooling now or ever."

We can't fool around with thoughts of self-pity, anger, resentment or hate. We can't fool around with thoughts of worry and fear. We can't fool around with any of these negative emotions because there is no fooling about the results. There is no fooling about the effects of every thought and feeling and every word. What we allow in our minds and hearts and what we let ourselves say, all come back to us, all come to fruition. We don't want to have the effects of fooling around.

We want to be sure that there is good of every kind in our lives and there can be, but good cannot come through our fooling around. We want others to come clear, we want children to behave. We want our thoughts and words and feelings to come clear. We want them to behave in the positive, all good, expecting way. Today we pray for God's helping us to stop any fooling around with the negative that we have been allowing. Today we're through with fooling around and we tell ourselves over and over, "No fooling around. What you're doing is for real. No fooling around."

## Taking Risks

Dear Friend,

Some of us try to avoid taking risks of any kind. Others of us will take almost any risk that presents itself as a possibility for improvement of any part of our life. There is danger in being too fast in accepting risks and there is danger in not taking any risks. It all depends on the risk. One risk we want to think about today is taking a risk in changing ourselves.

We do this whenever we take an objective view of ourselves and decide to change. It's so good for us to get objective about us so we really hear us talk, hear what we think and plan and want and watch us in action. We may not be satisfied with what we are seeing but we don't want to risk anything by changing. It is a risk. Perhaps we fear we can't change ourselves, or won't be comfortable in the new way of living. We think maybe it isn't really the good way we think now it will be, maybe we will fail and can't change, maybe other people won't approve. Besides we are so in the habit of being as we are, we are so used to all of our ways of responding to life.

It is a risk to change but when we know we need to, the risk is worth the taking. We can think of it as an investment not a speculation. We are investing our thinking and feeling and plans of action in becoming what we believe we should become. God will help us because God wants the best for us and wants us to be the best. Today we risk changing for the better and we change with God's help.

## Boomerangs

Dear Friend,

Today we think about boomerangs. Everything in life is a boomerang. Perhaps you and I had fun with a boomerang when we were children. We never got over the surprise of the way that boomerangs came back at us and we had to be very good at throwing it so that it would not come back and whack us. It could smart, so we learned to be careful. We are throwing boomerangs all the time.

Every thought we think, every word we speak, every emotion we express is a boomerang. They go out from us, we send them out. Sometimes we send them out with force as we think angry thoughts and shout angry words. Sometimes they go out gently as we are kind and considerate. However we send them out, they come back full circle. They always come back. We must remember this. What we send out comes back to us. The wonderful part is that we can choose what we send out.

We can choose the kind of boomerang we are going to be hit with for hit we will be. At times we wonder what hit us. If we are honest with ourselves, we will know that we are hit with what we have sent out. Then we can change. We don't have to get hit again and again. We can send out happy, loving things that come back softly, happily, lovingly. Today we look both to what we are sending out and what we are receiving. We remember *we* throw our boomerangs. With God's help we can send out only good ones.

## No Enemies

Dear Friend,

No man can be against me. No woman can be against me. The world cannot be against me. It may seem they can. It may seem that people and circumstances are against us. They will be if we think they are. They will be if we give them our permission to be against us. They can't really be against us because God is in us and God is all around us and God is in them and all around them.

There is no place for any deliberate hurting to be, any deliberate attempting to put obstacles in our paths. No place where God is not. Today we make this our theme song: "I can be no place where God is not. God is with me. God is all around me. No one is trying to hurt me. No one can be an enemy. No one can hurt me. God is with me in everything that I am doing. God is all around me protecting me. God is in me directing me. God is outside of me helping me. God is in others helping me. God in me is loving me. God in others is loving me. No one can be against me. God is for me and God is everywhere."

Today I remember this. No one can be against me. No one is against me. I stop thinking, "This is my enemy. This person is wanting to hurt me." Instead I say, "God in this person loves me. God in this situation is helping me, providing for me, blessing me, loving me." Today and every day we can be no place where God is not.

## No Ashes

Dear Friend,

Dear Abby says many wise things. One was that people who fight fire with fire usually end up with ashes. Oh, don't you and I know this is true! If someone speaks sharply to us and we speak sharply back, then the situation is worse. If one hits and the other hits back, both get hurt. Even in what we thought were fun stunts, playing practical jokes on one another often backfired. When we tried to get even with someone who had pulled one on us, things got out of hand and were no longer fun. Whenever we get an "I'm gonna show him (or her)" feling going, we'd better remember that if we fight fire with fire we're going to end up with ashes.

Somehow we have the illusion that if we can get even, we'll show the other person how great we are and that will make everything right. It makes everything wrong. Today let's look back a bit on our lives and see what happened the times we struck back, the times we set out to get even. That little bit more we thought that we were going to have became a whole lot more and not the kind we were after. Today let's pray to our Father-Mother God and ask for help in remembering this, in not even wanting to get even, to strike back, to make the other person pay in any way. It isn't worth it. We know from past experiences it is never worth it. When we let things go without retaliation, we have nothing to take care of ourselves. Today we don't fight fire with fire and we never have any ashes to clean up.

## Get the 'Let' Out

Dear Friend,

We are familiar with the expression to "get the lead out and get going" meaning we are to stop stalling and get going. The other day I heard someone use this phrase and I thought at first she was saying "get the let out" because we had been talking about the power of the Word of God and the creation as described in the first chapter of Genesis and we agreed that this was really what we should be doing, getting the "let there be's out," saying the Word, declaring the Word for whatever we need to have, need to change, need to bring about. Let there be.

God said, "Let there be" and there was. Too often we simply think about things that we want different or we want to add. We can be in an inharmonious situation. Instead of fretting about it, let us get that LET out, "Let there be peace and harmony." If we are experiencing lack of any kind, we get that LET out, "Let there be abundance." If we are lonely, we don't wallow in self-pity but get the LET out, "Let there be the friends, let there be activity for me." If we need a job, instead of despairing and feeling that no one wants us, out comes the LET, "Let there be the perfect job for me right now. Let there be."

No matter what it is that needs transformation in our lives, today we get the LET out and we decree, "Let there be good of every kind in my life and affairs right now." And there will be.

## No Rain on Your Parade

Dear Friend,

A friend of mine used an expression the other day that I had not heard before. It is a good one. "Don't let anyone rain on your parade." She told one of her sons this when he was unhappy over something that had occurred. Isn't it a wonderful picture? We can see a parade, the action, the crowds, the happiness, the expectancy, the music, floats, everyone out to have a good time.

Sometimes rain does come and can play havoc with costumes, flower arrangements, floats and all the crepe paper. Uniforms can lose their crispness, hairdos come down most unflatteringly. Perhaps we never saw a rained on parade but we can picture it in our minds. We know what would happen, how the parade would look and we think of the music. The bands would be practially stopped. Crowds would disappear.

Now, let's think, if someone had the power to turn off that rain, what a difference. People would come back, bands start playing, clothing dry, spirits soar, the parade would go on its merry, wonderful way. We have that needed power in our lives.

We can turn the rain on and we can turn it off. When we let others disappoint us, hurt our feelings, make us feel dejected, angry, impatient, any of the rainy kinds of feelings, we don't need to stay in the rain we have turned on. We have turned it on, we can turn it off.

144

## Moaner or Groaner?

Dear Friend,

Are we a moaner and a groaner? We can be a moaner and a groaner without making outer sounds. We can moan and groan inside. We are moaners and groaners if we constantly repeat what has happened, if we go over and over things we have allowed to make us unhappy. If we rehearse scenes of what has been. These may be scenes when we really tell someone off, they may be scenes of anger or hurt. Or they may be scenes of fear of what we think may be going to happen to us. We may dwell on our physical condition, our job condition, our money, our chidren, our parents, our neighbors.

We need to listen to ourselves as if we were someone else, someone eaves dropping on our thoughts and feelings. What would we hear? Moaning and groaning? Or hear a release from old things? Moaning and groaning take time and energy, time and energy that should be placed on the new and the good that lies ahead for everyone of us.

We stop wasting time moaning and groaning right now and give God the opportunity to work through us and for us. Gone will be anger, righteous indignation, gone will be sadness, gone will be fear, gone will be remorse, gone will be self-pity. Today with God's help we don't moan and groan.

## Running Away

Dear Friend,

A friend came by the other day to tell me goodbye. He was on his way out of town, bag and baggage. "I'm leaving it all behind. I'm going to start over." What he really was saying was, "I'm running away. I'm not facing what I should face." You and I can never run away to success and happiness if we have not taken care of what is where we are. We only kid ourselves.

This man needed to face a few people, say, "I was wrong. I was stupid. I've learned. I really regret it." Often when we don't want to face people or situations there is really nothing for us to fear. I knew but he would not listen that these people had no hard feelings about him, still believed in him. But he's running. You and I can have times when we feel like running, when we try to fool ourselves into thinking we can go somewhere else, be with some new people and the past will go away. The past does not go away until we face it, do what we can to make amends. That is the only way we can ever be free for new good. What we have done in the past continues until we face it. Starting new has nothing to do with the old.

Today, if there is anything we need to take care of in the past, let's pray for God guidance and help in facing it, in doing what we can about it now. We don't ever have to run and we pray, "Father-Mother God, thank You for helping me face my past and doing something about it. I know I will only lose if I run. With Your help, I don't have to run." And we don't. With God's help and our doing what we can, our past will be taken care of and we can go on victorious.

## Divine Timeliness

Dear Friend,

We think about Divine timeliness. Divine timeliness occurs when we let the divine in us, God in us, Christ in us, direct us so that we are always where we should be when we should be. Divine timeliness helps us get things done. Diving timeliness helps us meet people we should meet when we need to meet them or when they need to meet us. Happy things happen. Important to us things happen. We get in tune with the universe.

We are outside looking up when the heavens put on a spectacular display that lasts only a moment or two, but we see it. Cloud formations form for us, sunsets paint themselves for us, sun rays appear in all their splendor. The moon lights up our world. We meet someone who knows what we need to know, someone who can help us. We don't get exhausted in a divinely timed day because divine timeliness brings right periods of work and rest.

Today we take time to decree and let divine timeliness be ours. We pray, "Father-Mother God, I'm so glad, so very glad, that there is divine timeliness. I am one with it. I let it flow through me and my life. This is one of Your great gifts for me. Today I accept Your divine timeliness. Thank You."

Today is our day of divine timeliness.

## End of the Line

Dear Friend,

Today we think about release. We remember when we used to play crack the whip when we were children. We know what happened when we were at the end of the whirling line and were let go, We flew, we felt light. It was a happy exhilaration. We can have the same feeling when we let a problem go that has been holding us tight and that has been determining how we were to go even as that line of children in crack the whip held us until we were free.

Release exhilarates us. Because we know this, it is strange that we hang on to problems, keep thinking about them, keep stewing about them. We have said, "let go and let God." so often the words are only words now. They have no actual meaning to us, certainly no feeling of relief. That relief comes only with actual release, the complete letting go of whatever has been keeping us worried, afraid or angry. A complete letting go.

A letting go that means we are not going to think about it again, only long enough to tell our minds that we are through, tell our emotions that they can no longer use this to disturb us.

We can see our problem flying off, flying off to God's care. It is out of our hands. We release ourselves as we release our problem. We don't run after it. We let it go—to God.

## No More Clutter

Dear Friend,

Most of us can look about us and see clutter. We can look at our lives and see clutter. We can look inside us and see clutter. It's time to get order into our lives. We know we cannot operate effectively in clutter. We can let so much clutter happen. Order is mentioned many times in the Bible.

Abraham placed the wood in order for the sacrificial fire he thought he would have for his beloved son. God gave frequent directions for things to be set in order. Paul mentions order several times. We know order is essential so we start today to get order started so it will stay.

Order makes room, order saves mishaps, order saves time and effort. We pray, "Father-Mother God, thank You for Your orderly universe. Thank You for Your taking care of us in an orderly way. We know that with You all things happen at the right time, at the right place and in the right way. Today, dear Father-Mother God, I start to get order established. Thank You, Father, for helping me establish and then keep order established in my life and affairs."

Today is a day of order. We do not worry because we don't get everything orderly. We start order coming. Order will add to order until our lives are orderly. We give thanks that this is so.

## Time To See

Dear Friend,

Today we are not going to be too busy to see things, to hear things, to smell things, to touch, to taste, to sense. We can become so used to walking or driving a certain way that we do not see the special beauty of that drive. We can miss the beautiful cloud formations. Birds can sing their different songs, people can tell us things and we don't hear them. We can walk near roses or honeysuckle or abelia and not smell them. People are close and we don't touch. We eat too quickly. Today we don't.

We don't want to miss any of life and we have been missing so much. Today we will see all that God has for us to enjoy. We will see how much the young trees along the highway have grown. We will see children at play, hear their voices. We will be aware that our children want more than lunch money. We will be aware of what everyone wants or needs. We will take time to touch, to hug, to hold close. We wll not be so self engrossed that we do not know what is going on with other people.

*Today we are aware.* God has made us an instrument of awareness. Today we use all of our sensitivity to what is around us and to others around us and, as we do this, we will be more truly sensitive to ourselves. It will be a day of joy and beauty.

We say with deep feeling, "Today I am aware."

## Unimpressed

Dear Friend,

A helpful article I read the other day had for its title, "Unimpressed, Undisturbed." That's a terrific title. It carries a walloping truth. It is a wonderful way to tell us that we decide whether we are going to be affected by what others do or say or by what happens to us. If we do not let what others do or say, or, not do and we do not let circumstances make an imprint on our thinking and feeling, then nothing is going to happen. We will not be disturbed. We will not be unhappy. We will not be irritated. We will not be depressed. We will not be angry. We will not have our feelings hurt. We will not be afraid or resentful or guilty. What good words! We can practice saying to ourselves when things are not to our liking, "I am not impressed. Because I am not impressed I am not going to be disturbed, unhappy, angry or whatever could be the reaction if I allowed myself to be impressed by what has happened."

We will be like a film that went through the camera but came out still unexposed. so there was no picture. We go through experiences, we listen to things, things are done around us and to us but we go through them unimpressed by the negation and we come out undisturbed. We come through calm, serene, happy. We come through without any of the ill effects we might have had.

So today we say many, many times, whenever the temptation comes to react negatively, "I am unimpressed, I am undisburbed."

151

## Forgotten Dreams

Dear Friend,

Today we are going to think about all the dreams we have been pushing back. We must not lose our dreams. Dreams give purpose to life. Dreams of achievement, of improvement, of happiness, health, success, understanding come to us because there is in us a plan for our happiness, for our health, for our success, for our understanding and wisdom.

This is part of our creation, it is part of God in us, it is part of our individuality, our uniqueness, our specialness. Today we think of dreams we have almost forgotten because we have considered that they were only dreams. We call them only dreams because we think they are not possible. Dreams are possible. Dreams are from the very IN of us that tells us that these things are possible. When we start to love a dream again, start belieiving that a dream is possible for us, give new life to that dream, we start keeping it in our thoughts and feelings. Ideas will start coming from our Indwelling Lord telling us what we can do to help this dream become reality.

Today we remember our dreams, love these dreams, pray about them. We start nurturing our dreams so they come alive. They will.

## An Inside Job

Dear Friend,

We never have a problem outside of us. They are always inside us. There may be problems around us involving others but the ones we are involved with are ours to deal with inside us. How we deal with them on the inside of us determines how they develop on the outside.

Something happens that we do not like. If we react in anger, the outside gets worse. If we get at peace within ourselves, the situation outside changes. We face a situation that is fearful to us. It may be physical, it may be a relationship, it may be financial. We take care of the fear inside us first. We remember that greater is God within us than anything outside us. We remember that we are pomised angels to go before us and that God is love and love is in us to enjoy and to express and we find we know what to do. We find help coming to us. Inside we find courage and strength we didn't know we had. Inside we find wisdom we didn't know we had. Inside we find solutions we had not thought possible. Inside we find greater joy than we have had before. Today we look inside first. Whatever we face today must be first faced inside. How wonderful we can do something ourselves. We do not have to depend on others.

## Seeing God

Dear Friend,

Today we are going to see God in us, God in others, God in everything. We believe God is omnipresent, everywhere equally present.

If God is in all people and in all things, it's about time you and I start seeing God in others, in happenings, in places and things and in ourselves. Often the very last place we look for God is in us, but God has to be. There's no place for God to stop being. There's no place for God to start or end. God is. We start today to see God everywhere.

We have to decide to see God in the breeze, God in the clouds, in the leaves of the newly greened trees, God in the roses, God in people's faces, God in our work, God in buildings, God in fields and hills, rivers and creeks, God in animals, God in machinery, cars, traffic. We can be no place God is not. We cannot ever be without God in us.

God is always in us despite the anger, the resentment, the sadness, the hurt. God is here. We look to God in us and anger melts, resentment cools, sadness lifts, hurt heals. When we look to God in us, God in us can act, can show our God Self. When we look to God in others the same things happen. Things respond to our looking to God in them. When we look to see God in the world, the world is different. It will not stay a world filled with hatred and greed. It will become a caring world, a rich world, a happy world. We help the world. We see God everywhere.

## Jealousy Out

Dear Friend,

Sometimes we have a twinge of jealousy and we don't like it. Jealousy is one of the most painful emotions we can have. It can make us sick, it can make us do and say things we regret. Not one of us wants to be jealous, none of us want to be in the clutches of that green-eyed monster that does nothing but destroy. Jealousy destroys relationships, health, careers, even lives. And what is jealousy but self-discontent?

Jealousy is a feeling of inadequacy, a feeling of not being wanted, of not being good enough, a feeling that someone is stealing from us and we are not able to prevent it, a feeling of weakness, defenselessness. Our letting jealousy take over does not get rid of these feelings, only intensifies them so we go back to the cause—discontent with ourselves and feeling inadquate.

We stop feeling deprived and we remind ourselves firmly, perhaps sharply, so we will really hear, "I am adequate. I am a special person. I am able. I am a desirable person. I am me, the me God created as God created no one else. I have my special God given Self, my special abilities, attractiveness, goodness, intelligence, everything. I do not forget them. I am going to be the best me I can be.

"I do not have time to be jealous. I am not jealous."

## Joy to the World

Dear Friend,

We sing, "Joy to the world the Lord has come." We should feel this every morning and throughout the day. Our Lord is come, our Lord has come, our Lord is with us to stay for always and always. No waiting. No longing. Only a knowing that our Lord is here. Only an acceptance of this Truth about us. And it is a joyous Truth and is joy to our world, joy to all the world. Everything gets better for us when we know this. Everything gets better about us and every thing is helped toward getting better in all the world. We all know how wonderful it is to feel happy, happy inside us.

Something beautiful, light, wonderful starts to flow up through us. It is joy. The most wonderful happy thing that can happen to you and to me today is letting joy well up in us. It will as we acknowledge the Lord of our being as our king of kings, our helper, our teacher, our director, our guide, our provider, our everything. We've known this, perhaps only partially, but we've known it. Now we think about it, now we give thanks for it, now we remember it all day, now we sing about it. We sing the joys we are feeling. We sing our joy to the world about it. We sing it with love to others. We sing with understanding, with expectancy of good not only from and for ourselves but for others. We sing it for the world. We sing and sing and sing, "Joy to the world, the Lord has come. My Lord has come. Your Lord has come. Yes, joy to the world, the Lord is here now."

## Twenty-Third Psalm

Dear Friend,

The beauty and the promise of the 23rd Psalm has made it one of the most familiar of the Psalms. Many people have memorized it. Many people carry a copy of it in their billfolds. It has been a comfort and an inspiration, an assurance and a joy. It is the one Psalm that more of us know as a whole Psalm. However, there is so much more for us to gain from it when we think about each of its statements separately. The next thirteen letters are about them.

## I Have a Shepherd

Dear Friend,

The 23rd Psalm is filled with promises. Let's take it as our own personal Psalm and consider each statement by itself. The Psalm David sang begins, "The Lord is my shepherd." Five words. Five words of comfort, assurance, trust.

A shepherd takes care of his sheep. A shepherd provides for his sheep. A shepherd protects his sheep. A shepherd sees that there is food and a safe place for his sheep. A shepherd does everything necessary for the sheep's well-being. We have a Shepherd.

We have a Shepherd that will provide for us, lead us in safe ways, lead us to success and happiness, protect us from any kind of danger either physical or imaginary. A Shepherd who will provide food and shelter, whatever we need. Our Shepherd is the Lord of our being. The Lord who indwells us and who is everywhere present, the Lord who knows all and can do all. We have our Indwelling Lord who is with us all of the time, always has been with us, always will be with us. This Lord wants to help us, wants to provide for us.

We say the words and we sing the words: "The Lord is my Shepherd. The Lord is my Shepherd . . . . The Lord is my Shepherd." What wonderful words. The Father-Mother Within is my Shepherd.

# No Lack

Dear Friend,

Today we are going to use the second wonderful statement of the 23rd Psalm, "I shall not want." I shall not lack any good thing. I shall not be hungry. I shall not need money or lack a job. I shall not despair of better health. I shall not be unhappy. I shall not feel any lack of friends or love. I shall not want or need any good thing. How wonderful to contemplate a time when we shall not be wanting anything, will not be lacking anything.

Oh, we will always want some things but not because we feel we can't have them or that we are deprived or limited. It will not be a wanting to fill a desperate need. It will be a desire and a desire we know we can have filled because we will know from experience that we shall not want. No, we shall not lack any good thing and, if the desired is a good thing, it will come to us. Let's think about us.

Many of us have known what it is to want, to need food, to need clothing, to need a job, to need friends. And now we are affirming the words that David must have learned the truth of or he would not have been able to say them so beautifully. We are saying that now, today, right now, all want, all lack is going to end. We think what a difference in our lives. How different others' lives will be when they too know the wonder of this assurance.

They will not want. They will not lack. I shall not want. We shall not want today. We shall not want tomorrow. We shall not ever want. We give thanks to our Father-Mother God that this is so.

# Green Pastures

Dear Friend,

Today we are ready for the third affirmative statement of the 23rd Psalm, and we are going to have a wonderful day using the assuring words, "He makes me lie down in green pastures." We think first about sheep.

They have been grazing from the first light of the day. It gets hot. The shepherd finds a cool place, perhaps in the shade of some trees. The shepherd will try to find tall grass, grass that is green and soft so that the sheep will be comfortable. More than that, more than having grass that will be restful, we think of comfortable sleep for the sheep in the midst of plenty of food. Green pastures, comfortable pastures, restful pastures, abundant pastures, assurance of protection and plenty. What could be more wonderful? We can have the same feeling.

We can go to sleep at night knowing we are lieing down in our own green pastures. Rest is assured. Provision is assured. Our troubles are nothing. They can be taken care of. We can rest undisturbed. We are being watched over. We are being loved. We are being taken care of. We are comfortable. We can sleep undisturbed.

In the day time we can withdraw to our green pasture, if only in our mind. We can find rest and whatever supply we need. Our Shepherd will take care of us, God will take care of us.

We say many times today and, as we say the words, we think and feel and picture our own green pasture. "He makes me like down in green pastures." God makes me lie down in green pastures. God gives me my green pasture where I rest secure in God's all providing love.

## Still Waters

Dear Friend,

The words of the 23rd Psalm we are saying today are, "He leads me beside the still waters." What a picture this brings to our mind. It is a delightful picture of coolness and refreshing water. It brings us memory of the wonder of cool waters in the heat. Water is refreshing to us when we drink it, when we bathe in it, when we see it, when we are in it or on it. Still waters are peaceful waters. Our lives are not always peaceful.

They may not be full of friction or controversy but they may be unpeaceful from all of the activity in them. We need the stillness. We need to think about still waters. Our minds can become still pools even if they are filled with jumping thoughts. We may see our mind as a pool, a pond, a tank. We may see it as a river, bay or ocean. It doesn't matter what our picture is, not the size, color, not even the sky above. We see still waters.

What a beautiful sound the words have. In themselves there is stillness. And, as we say them and think them, we start to feel the stillness in us. Our thoughts calm, our emotions slow down. We become at peace, at ease.

Our Indwelling Lord is leading us beside still waters and we are being restored. We are at peace and we give thanks to our Father-Mother Within for leading us beside the still waters when we need stillness. Our Father-Mother ever waits to take us to the still waters and we go.

## Restoring Soul

Dear Friend,

It is refreshing to use this affirmative statement from the 23rd Psalm, "He restores my soul." We often have times when we feel that all of us is hurt, all is sick, all of us depleted. We feel not only fatigued in mind and body but tired in the very soul of us. We feel there is no part of us that is alive, that we have no enthusiasm for anything. And then we hear these words, "He restores my soul."

We know that when the inner of us is happy, then the body, mind and emotions can be too. We need our soul restored, we need the core of us restored, loved, appreciated, strengthened. These words assure us. These words tell us that what we need we will have, our soul will be restored. There is nothing said about asking for it, nothing about begging for it. Only the very plain words that the Lord will restore our soul. This is a wonderful promise. No more despair, no more despondency, no more inadequacy, no more emptiness. Our soul is to be restored.

Our soul is to be restored, and we pray, "Father-Mother God, thank You for restoring my soul. With my soul restored, all else is possible and all else will be right. Thank You." We go about our day singing inside. We have to sing! This is so wonderful to know. We sing and sing, "The Lord of my being, my own Indwelling Lord, restores my soul. Life is possible again. I am possible. Everything is possible. My soul is restored." We think and feel the wonder of it, the wonder of the restoring of our soul.

## Right Use

Dear Friend,

There is beautiful encouragement in these words from the 23rd Psalm, "He leads me in paths of righteousness for His name's sake." We think first what righteousness means. It is not an unattainable holiness or even an austere way of life. Righteousness means only right use of our talents, right use of our strength, right use of our time, right use of our life. We want to make right use of everything we have.

"For His name's sake." We know we have God's name. God said His name is "I Am" and that is our name. God's name and ours are the same. We are made in the image and likeness of God so we are called by the same name. When we are making right use, the best use of what we are and can be, then this will make us live up to our name, live up to our I Am name. It is for the sake of our I Amness that we are to be led in paths of right use of all we are.

This opens us up to letting more and more of our divine plan unfold. We relax any feeling of strain about what we are today. God, our Lord, the I Am of us, will lead us in the way we should go in order for us to live up to our I Am nature. And we pray, "Father-Mother God, thank You for giving me my own special abilities and thank You for leading me into the right use of them. Thank You for helping me live up to my name, I Am." And God will help us.

## Newness Comes

Dear Friend,

The passage from the 23rd Psalm, "Yea, though I walk through the valley of the shadow of death, I will fear no evil for thou are with me . . .," has had a mournful meaning for many people. There are many things in our lives that die. There may be a job death, a relationship death, an idea death, the death of a dream. If we know that God is with us we know that these deaths cannot be the end. The dream will revive or there will be another better and more wonderful dream. The idea is gone but, God with us, there will be many, many more ideas. A relationship ends. We give thanks for what has been and know that God will make the sorrow less difficult, because God is with us, there will be healing, there will be a softening of despair, and there will be something very good to fill what is a vacuum now.

The dead job will be only history, not the end of our achievement. There will be another job, another career possibility. God with us will find it for us, will bring a new and better job to us. Physical problems that threaten can change as we know God is with us. No matter what may seem the valley of the shadow of death, we can know it is not the end. God is with us. We will be all right and we give thanks that this is so.

## Needed Strength

Dear Friend,

What strength and assurance comes with today's study of the 23rd Psalm. "Your rod and Your staff comfort me." Rods and staffs are used for many things. Here they are symbolic. A rod helps us if the road is rough. A staff usually is pictured with a hooked neck. This gives us both the strength of a rod with the added possibility of hanging on to safety or bringing something to us. If we are thinking of ourselves as sheep with God as our shepherd, the Lord's staff can get hold of us and pull us back from danger. The Lord's rod will sound out the path for us, telling us where it is safe to go.

There is a rich feeling of safety in the rod and the staff. What can there be to fear if our Lord's rod and staff are ready to guide and protect us? Then the word comfort. It is such a good word, such a happy word. Comfort means to feel secure, to feel loved, to feel at ease, to feel there is nothing at all to fear or be concerned about. God's staff, God's strength, God's rod comfort us when we accept their availability.

We pray, "Father-Mother God, thank You for Your rod and Your staff. You keep me from going the wrong way with Your staff. Your rod, dear God, and Your staff make me comfortable in all of my activity today."

## Victory Dinner

Dear Friend,

The 23rd Psalm's "You prepare a table for me in the presence of my enemies," gives us a picture of victory. People may have been enemies but our Heavenly Father is preparing a special meal for us, a dinner of victory.

We can also see this as preparation for victory. Our Father-Mother is providing everything we need to overcome our enemies. Food represents strength. It represents whatever we need for our encounter with the enemy and for our coming out of our encounters victorious. Our enemies can be many. Our enemies can be only inside us.

One inner enemy is feeling unworthy. How can we be unworthy if our God prepares a table for us? Perhaps our enemy is fear. How can we fear with God our ever present protection? Perhaps doubt, but how can we doubt when we recognize all the good God has for us? Perhaps loneliness, but how can we be lonely if God is giving us all the good we need and is always with us? Guilt? God has to have forgiven us if God is preparing a victory banquet for us. Disappointment or hurt feelings? They dissolve in the richness of recognition of our worth by our Father-Mother God. God prepares a table of rich good for us in the presence of all our inner enemies and they slink away. We are refreshed. We are renewed. Our Father supports us.

## We're Special

Dear Friend,

"You anoint my head with oil." The 23rd Psalm becomes part of us as we spend time with it in prayer. We think what the word anoint means and we know that it means to set apart, to mark as special, to signify that specialness is expected of the anointed. We think about head, this is the top of us, this is the part of us that has our eyes, our ears, our taste, our smell, our brain through which we exercise our dominion of choosing thoughts and emotions, through which comes our inspiration, our ideas, through which we maintain consciousness. And we think of oil, always the symbol of love, of harmony, of smoothness, of easing friction, of soothing. So we know that God thinks we are special, that we have special things to do and we are going to be able to do them and that we are loved and we will be a harmonizer as well as a doer. Today we think about this.

God anoints us, anoints our head with oil, anoints us with love, peace and harmony. We have been especially set apart. We are special. We have a special work to do. We have our own mission. We have our own destiny and we have whatever we need and we have it all with love. How beautiful.

We pray, "You, my Father-Mother God, anoint my head with oil. You set me apart. You set me apart as special. I am special. You made me so and You give me all the ideas and strength, whatever is needed, and You give with love and You anoint with love."

Today we begin to realize that our specialness is so special that God anoints us with the oil of His love. How grateful we are.

## Overflowing Cup

Dear Friend,

"My cup runs over." We like full cups of anything good. These words from the 23rd Psalm tell us that our Father-Mother God has so much good for us that no cup can hold it. However, our God, our Supplier, our Giver of Good can give us only what we open up to accept. We are the cup. We are the receptacle for good in our lives. God fills us to overflowing if we expect and accept.

Always there is more than we have expected, always more beautiful, richer, happier good than we have even thought about. As children want large Christmas stockings to hang so that there will be room for more and larger gifts, we want to make ourselves the largest possible cup for our Father-Mother God to fill. We think of ourselves as cups that can hold life, energy, health, strength, vigor, vitality and hold ourselves open for the running over of life's goodness.

We picture our finances, our checkbooks and purses as cups all open to the bounty of God and we see God filling them to overflowing. We think of our joy as a cup and we open up so that our joy cup overflows with the beauty of new joys. We think of the entirety of our life as a cup. We hold it out for God to fill. Your cup and my cup can run over and they can continue to overflow with rich good.

## Goodness Forever

Dear Friend,

Let's take the last verse of the 23rd Psalm in two parts. There is much in each part, such beautiful promises, so beautiful, so wonderful that we need to savor each part by itself and the magnitude of the two together can be more completely felt. Today, "Surely goodness and mercy shall follow me all the days of my life." Goodness we can think of as all kinds of good—happiness, health, wisdom, prosperity, everything that feels good to us. Goodness is people to love us, people to be with us, understanding, a good feeling about ourselves, the goodness of feeling God in us and all around us. Goodness is having enough for all our needs. Goodness is good people to be with, good work to do, recognition, success. The list is long, the promise is broad. Goodness, goodness, everything we call good to follow us, to be ready for us all the days of our lives. And there will also be mercy.

We will be dealt with compassionately, understandingly, be forgiven if we need forgiving, given another chance when we need it. Above all we will be understood, loved. How magnificent!

Oh, what life holds for us when we contemplate this promise. Only goodness is coming, nothing else is coming to us, only goodness and mercy, only all we need materially, emotionally, spiritually. All the understanding we need, all the forgiveness, only goodness for us, only mercy. What a future.

It is sure, for "Surely goodness and mercy will follow me all the days of my life." And we give thanks.

169

## God's House Our House

Dear Friend,

Today we think about the last verse of the 23rd Psalm, "I will dwell in the house of the Lord forever." This is the Truth about us.

We are dwelling in the house of the Lord right now. The Lord is dwelling in us right now. God with us. God in us. We are with God. We live forever with God. We are ever in God's Presence. Whatever house means to us, God is there. Whatever we think of house as being, it is God's house. Our family structure, our apartment, permanent homes, temporary homes, overnight homes, homes we visit, buildings we work in, wherever we are, it is God's and we are living there and we are living there forever.

Our bodies are temples, houses for our Indwelling Lord. God is ever in them, we ever in them. There is no place for us to be except in the house of the Lord for all is our Lord's and we are His. We can no longer feel homeless, rejected. We can no longer feel separated in any way from our good. We are dwelling now in God's house. We are God's house and this is forever not for a few moments, not for a few days but forever.

The whole 23rd Psalm sings to us and it sings in rising wonder and beauty until it reaches this beautiful Truth about us. We are living in the house of the Lord, and we will dwell in the house of the Lord forever and in that house is all possibility, all good, all health, all love, all happiness—forever.

## Mists Lift

Dear Friend,

On a misty dark morning there seemed to be little promise of light coming, although I knew light, full light would come soon. Then as I continued to look up, all of a sudden there was gold on the very top tips of the trees ahead of me. Where that golden light was there was no mist. There was mist above and below but not in the light. A promise of the sureness of the coming light, beautiful light, golden light.

There are misty times in our lives, times when there seems only darkness but we keep our vision high. I would have missed this tree top glow had I been looking down at the ground. We can miss the light that promises us that our darkness is already starting to dissipate and our light is already starting to come. We see this light when we look up, when we raise up our consciousness, raise up our faith, raise up our expectation of good, expectation of the solution to problems, expect healings. If we keep our attention only on the darkness we are walking through, if we feel only the mistiness of uncertainty and allow that to become discouragement, dread, fear, then we miss the glow, we miss the promise of the dawn of new and wonderful and very beautiful good that is coming to us. So, we pray, "Father-Mother God, I keep my vision high. I know the dawn is coming, I know my good is coming. Thank You for showing me the first golden signs of the new dawn in my life." And God will.

## Seeing God's Image

Dear Friend,

Today we look at ourselves in a new way. When we catch a glimpse of ourselves in mirrors or plate glass windows, we will see a new person. We will not see us as we have been.

We will look at ourselves seeing the image of our Creator in whose likeness we were created. No matter what we have allowed to happen to our physical selves or to our lives we remember today we are created in God's image. It can help if we say to ourselves, "I am the image and likeness of God. I am. I really am the image and likeness of God." As we say this and we think of ourselves this way, we will start seeing changes.

Things about us that we have been not pleased with will no longer seem permanent. The God image of us will seem possible. As we see ourselves as God's image and likeness, we call forth the God potential that is in us, and we begin to look different, we will begin to feel different, and we will be different. We start to let that image come forth. It will and we will start to express God in all we do. We will express God's love, wisdom, caring, strength, health, vitality, love and niceness. Our experiences will change. All our life will change for the better.

Today we joyously tell ourselves that we are the image and likeness of God and that image now shows to us and to others.

### I Carry Peace

Dear Friend,

*Wherever I am, there is peace.* First, we have to be at peace because we cannot give what we don't have. We become still. We remember Jesus the Christ left us His peace, a peace deeper, greater, more wonderful and lasting than any peace the world knew.

This is the peace we want. This is the peace that is ours to have and to enjoy, the peace that we are to have so that we can share it, so that we can bring peace wherever we are, can bring peace to others.

*Wherever I am today there is peace.* Right now where I am there is peace because I am at peace. *I am at peace. I am at peace. I am at peace with myself.* I am at peace with all of my loved ones. I am at peace with friends, with business associates, with clients, students, customers, co-workers. *I am at peace. I am at peace.*

*I am filled with God's peace. I am filled with God's peace. I am filled with God's peace.* Peace is in me and through me. It pours out to bless the world. It is as if I had a long cloak of peace. I am enveloped in peace. I envelop others in peace. My robe of peace flows out and out. I am filled with peace. Wherever I am there is peace.

How wonderful!

Never forget, dear Friend,

God loves you,

You are loved,

and

I love you,

Mary Katherine

Other books by Mary Katherine MacDougall:

*Black Jupiter*
*What Treasure Mapping Can Do For You*
*Prosperity Now*
*Healing Now*
*Happiness Now*
*Making Love Happen*